The Psychic Housewives' Handbook

The Psychic Housewives' Handbook

★

Lorraine Roe

HAMPTON ROADS
PUBLISHING COMPANY, INC.

Cover design by Adrian Morgan
Cover art by © istockphoto

Hampton Roads Publishing Company, Inc.
1125 Stoney Ridge Road
Charlottesville, VA 22902

434-296-2772
fax: 434-296-5096
e-mail: hrpc@hrpub.com
www.hrpub.com

If you are unable to order this book from your local
bookseller, you may order directly from the publisher.
Call 1-800-766-8009, toll-free.

Library of Congress Cataloging-in-Publication Data

Roe, Lorraine, 1963-
The psychic housewives' handbook : how to keep your feet on the
ground and your head in the stars / Lorraine Roe.
      p. cm.
   Summary: "A guide on how to awaken latent psychic abilities,
specifically targeting women"–Provided by publisher.
   ISBN 978-1-57174-598-9 (5.5 x 8.5 tp : alk. paper)
   1. Women–Psychic ability. I. Title.
   BF1045.W65R64 2009
   133.8082–dc22
                                             2008051455

ISBN 978-1-57174-598-9

10 9 8 7 6 5 4 3 2 1

Printed on acid-free paper in the United States

Contents

Foreword

✦✦By Echo Bodine✦✦

There couldn't be a more perfect time for this book to be published. With all the old souls being born in the last ten to fifteen years, many gifted children are asking their moms lots of questions for which they may not have the answers.

The topic? Psychic abilities and all that goes along with them.

Lorraine is an exceptional psychic, writer, mom, and housewife who recognized, through her own gifted children, the needs of this new generation and also the quandary that many moms are facing today. If the world continues to go in the current direction, the parents of tomorrow need to help their kids with some unique additions to reading, writing and 'rithmetic. More than ever before, children are communicating with their spirit guides, remembering past lives, and seeing the future. If you have such a child, my guess is that you are also blessed with these abilities but for one reason or another have never looked into it.

If this is the case, this is an excellent book for you because it will help you to understand your gifts and give you guidance on helping your children with theirs.

I have seen Lorraine's abilities blossom over the last ten years, and she is an excellent psychic. She has been through it all and knows what she's talking about.

Here are some of the key points that she covers in this book:

* meditation as a tool in developing your relationship with your inner voice
* open relationships with your spirit guides
* tools to release old patterns that keep you stuck and unable to realize your gifts
* psychic protection and how to avoid the energy vampires in your life
* important ingredients in being a professional psychic
* permission to make a fool of yourself and put your ego in check
* boundaries and ethics about being a professional psychic
* trust in your inner voice as a guide for living

If you are a psychic housewife, your days are filled to the brim with more than you can handle, but this is an important part of you that we're talking about. As you learn about your own potential, you'll be able to answer your children's questions about the unique aspects of their world:

* invisible friends
* dearly departed Grampa sitting at the dinner table
* pretty colors around people
* fairies

Foreword

Lorraine's quick wit and straightforward manner are a breath of fresh air, so make yourself a cup of tea, put your feet up, and let her teach you all about the gifts you already have.

Acknowledgments

Even though I believe in reincarnation, I know I'm only going around once in this body. The people in my past and present have shaped me into the author before you now. I better thank them while I have the chance.

Thank you to my husband, Jon. People who first meet you always think you're a nice guy. You're not. You're tough and don't put up with manipulation or deceit. You are also amazingly generous, loving, and easygoing with your family, friends, and coworkers. I love all the sides of your personality. Thanks for all the laughs. You are a funny, incredibly creative, wonderful husband and dad. I like your style; it keeps away the riffraff. Thanks, honey, for being you and helping me bridge the gap from reporter to psychic. Have I told you recently how good you look on your Harley?

To my children, Kendall, Nathan, and Sam—I am so blessed to have you in my life. You've shaped me into a loving mom. I am so grateful every day for the blessed time we have together. I believe we honor each other every day with our laughter, tears, and love.

And thank you to Madeleine for your messages from heaven. I believe you when you say you are the *L* in Lorraine.

A special thank you to my spirit helpers. You're funny, sexy, and comforting, but not codependent. I like that in an angel.

Thank you to Greg Brandenburgh at Hampton Roads Publishing for knowing when to say no, when to say yes, and for being ridiculously enthusiastic. Five years ago, you told me I had a book in me—and here it is, thanks to you!

Thank you to everyone else at Hampton Roads Publishing for your wonderful work and your help with this book.

Thank you to psychic and teacher Echo Bodine. Your humor and wisdom helped me to keep my sanity through all the rapid changes. Your referrals have helped to keep me afloat financially. Your love and talent have helped so very many. The people I do readings for tell me that about your work all the time. I couldn't agree more.

Where would I be without my girlfriends? Going nowhere fast, that's where. Thank you to Helen Michaels for teaching me the power of being gentle and carrying a big stick. It took a Southern woman to set me straight on that topic. You are a gift, a heavenly channel, and a dear friend. I truly believe this psychic journey would not have been possible without you. I want to thank my friend Annelise Christ. You took a very raw version of this book and shaped it into something worth reading. Your insights, friendship, and energy never cease to amaze me. We've known each other for a long time, Annelise, and our friendship just keeps getting better. THANK YOU! Thank you to Susan Gustafson. Even though you're in Africa helping the orphans, I often feel as though you are standing right next to me. Thank you for more than two decades of steadfast friendship. Thank you to Toni Callahan for standing by me through thick and thin. Your humor always feels like a life raft. A special mention goes to Mindy Miller. We have been friends since third grade when I raised my hand to have you sit next to me. You have taught me the power of honest communication and asking for what you want in a friendship. To Miranda Barrett, thanks for being a fellow healer who's willing to climb all sorts of mountains! This next phase is going to be so fun! Thanks to my friends Michelle and Lynne. Hello to Leslie Tolon. You are a tough cookie, a wonderful mom, and a sweet friend. Thanks to Jennifer Bigelow for your wit and wisdom.

Thank you to Alex for Kendall and Nathan and the great job you do as their father. Thank you for the life lessons and your humor. Good luck with the Chihuahuas!

I thank my stepmom, Doris, and my dad, Ken, for teaching me why it is important to clean the house every day and for showing me the value of nature, respectively. I didn't understand either very well until I had kids of my own. Thanks to my dad for telling me why eating ice cream every day makes you jaded. I've never forgotten.

Thank you to my other family members in Redding, California, for your love and support.

Thanks to my mother-in-law Barbara for being my mom away from home. Having you with us when Sam was born meant the world to me.

I had the privilege of spending a lot of time with all four of my grandparents into my late thirties. I thank each of them for teaching me the power of unconditional love.

I thank my mother, Joan, who's hanging in heaven and has been there for most of my adult life. Thanks for telling me that you can be psychic without being crazy.

Thank you to the McAdams side of the family. Without you, I'm not sure where I'd be now. We've all had our share of insanity. But I'm sure none of us have laughed harder than when we're all in one room together.

Thanks to all my psychic friends, clients, students, and YouTube viewers—you rock!

Thanks to Trino for the laughs and support ever since our Savannah days.

Hello to Robb and the former news gang at Channel Five.

Hello to our friends in Fort Jones and Mt. Shasta!

And finally to my loyal dog, Vesta, thank you for your patience this summer while I was wrapping up the book. I know I owe you hundreds of hours at dog park and some quality time up north. Years before we met, I had a vision of a black and white dog licking my face. When I met you, that dream came true. You're more dog than anyone could ask for.

Lorraine Roe
08/08/08

✦Chapter 1✦
Suddenly Psychic! What a Trip!

It began with a grandma. She wasn't mine and she wasn't alive. The gray-haired woman showed me a boy wearing a striped shirt, holding a bucket filled with peaches. The boy had sandy-colored hair and a sweet expression on his face. He was standing on a porch near an orchard. Her energy was pushing the imagery into my head and I could feel in my stomach her fondness for the boy. As I sat at my desk at home, the mental picture was crystal clear. Later I brought it up to a doctor friend of mine. I sensed the woman I had seen was his grand-mother. He confirmed my suspicions. He told me he had recently been looking at an old photo of that very scene taken some forty years ago. It was a black and white photo of him, holding a peach bucket at his grand-mother's home by an orchard.

The incident happened in my late thirties. I had never had anything quite like that happen to me before. After the dead grandma visited me, I was never the same. I went from being a hard-charging skeptical television reporter to a professional psychic in about a year. Need-less to say, my former news coworkers found it quite shocking. Frankly, so did I.

I had made some significant changes in my life in the several years before I saw and heard from my friend's deceased grandma. I had spent two years doing daily meditation and yoga, had read numerous books about spiritual development, and had quit my job as a news reporter. That afternoon experience with the grandmother spirit was the start of many full-blown psychic experiences. Soon I was seeing ghosts and spirit guides and having visions of what was going to happen next, on a regular basis. Prior to this, I had received mental images of future situations in my life, but this was different. This was seeing and hearing about details from other people's lives, details I could not possibly have known without psychic insight. It is a phenomenon that is happening to countless people. I have met them and heard their stories.

Many students in my psychic development classes arrive truly believing they are not psychic. Within twelve weeks, they are giving accurate psychic information to each other. They are also hearing and following divine guidance with amazing results. I have also seen dear friends open up psychically in sudden and magical ways. In this book, you will hear from some of my students and friends. You may have similar psychic experiences while reading it. And you have probably already had many amazing coincidences in your own life involving your intuition. By taking a few simple steps on a daily basis, you can resuscitate your full psychic abilities. Let's call it psychic ability 911. An emergency crew is coming to give life support to the invisible force that supports you best. Imagine this crew breathing life back into your divine knowing and your self-care. Your true psychic self is waiting for you in the future. She is asking you to bone up on your skills, to fulfill your destiny.

For me, becoming a psychic housewife has been a journey through many worlds. I have learned to ruthlessly follow my gut, sometimes to the point of feeling like a drowning woman. Somehow, a life preserver always shows up at the last minute. How's that for sugarcoating the journey? Spirit is a tease, asking you to take risks on its behalf. The journey is dangerous and loaded with pitfalls. But the rewards are thrilling. In the end you are stronger and more content for having taken the journey. On a more mundane level, you may find yourself knowing your waitress's thoughts while you're out to dinner or realizing that one of your friends is dating the wrong guy because you can read his energy. You might also notice the ghost in the corner, the one bothering your kids and making the house feel uncomfortable. These are real experiences of women who have become psychic. It can be fun, it can be scary, and it can seem unreal. But it can also feel like coming home, back to the you that you really are. It can feel like absolute truth.

Throughout my life, I have had psychic experiences. At the time I had them, however, I did not define them that way. Years ago, for example, when I was working as a television reporter in Savannah, Georgia, I woke up one morning as a voice told me I was going to meet a pilot. I had no idea what to make of this, so I just got up and went to work. I reported a story at the local military base about servicemen being overseas for Thanksgiving. I then left and drove by a man walking on a traffic island on the base. Something told me to offer him a ride. When he was in the car, he told me he was a navy pilot and had tried to fly home to California to surprise his family for Thanksgiving. His plane had mechanical difficulties, though, so he was going to miss spending the holiday with them. I ended up inviting him to my home that evening, where a bunch of coworkers and their families were gathering to celebrate Thanksgiving. He attended and later sent me a letter saying how much the invitation meant to him. At the time, I could barely believe the "coincidence." Now I understand that his guides were taking care of him by reaching out to me.

In my career as a television reporter, I had an uncanny ability to find different sources to tell me about the same story, to arrive at a story location exactly when the action was happening, and to break big local news stories with ease. It would infuriate my management that I would wait until late in the morning to leave the newsroom with the photographer and get my interviews and video. But there was almost always a complete flow and synchronicity that happened once I was in the field.

Once when I was working on a story in Minneapolis, one of my sources commented on my impeccable timing. The seasoned news photographer raised his eyebrow and told the source, "We like to think of her as a witch in the newsroom." Ha, very funny. Looking back now, I can see how there were many, many guides and angels helping with the timing of the stories and whispering in my ear about sources and ideas. In fact, it was very witch-like. It was pure magic.

In my personal life, I had premonitions about running into people, about gifts I would receive, and even about the imminent death of a loved one.

One week before I was due to deliver my first baby, I

was talking to a dear friend. "Can you believe it?" she said. "In another week you'll be home with your baby girl."

From out of nowhere, I had the thought, "No, I won't." I saw myself sitting in the baby rocker alone, crying.

At the time, I shuddered and brushed it off—something I would not do now. One week after that vision, I delivered my stillborn baby. It was heartbreaking. But looking back, I see that in one brief moment, spirit was preparing me for what was ahead.

I had several isolated incidents that seemed to involve "seeing" other dimensions. One experience that was rather jolting happened with a friend on a weekend trip to the desert. We both saw sparkling dust falling from the ceiling of a vacation home we were renting. We also saw ghosts at the same time. When we were both seeing demon spirits racing around on the ceiling, my friend revealed that he was psychic, which I hadn't known. And in case you are wondering, I was stone cold sober at the time. I marveled at these isolated perceptions, but did not think of them as psychic experiences.

The more I hear from clients and friends, the more I laugh at how obvious the psychic realm can be, but how often we go into a state of denial to avoid feeling "psychic." Many of us have had experiences such as premonitions, seeing ghosts, or hearing the voice of an angel whisper in our ear. When you add up the pieces, it looks an awful lot like psychic ability. Those smaller pieces connect to create a large landscape puzzle called the psychic realm. When you begin to relax about the notion and realize these abilities want and deserve your time and attention, the magic happens. Years ago, I finally gave in and dove into books about psychic ability. I learned to meditate and I began consciously listening to and following my inner guidance. Within two years, I was seeing and hearing from dead people on a regular basis. And the angelic voices came in much more clearly.

As psychic housewives, we live in a world of kids, laundry, carpooling, and part-time work. It is also a world of strange coincidences, ghosts, spirit guides, and even a few spaceships and aliens. Many moms have crossed my path with their feet on the ground and their heads in the stars. To be more precise, they have their hands in dishwater while their ears are tuned to a heavenly frequency.

Often the first to lead these moms on their spiritual paths are their own children. While working as a professional psychic, I have met quite a few moms because their kids were talking about seeing ghosts or fairies. Our children don't have the same filters we do. They see it and they believe it. There are many common themes people want answers for when consulting a psychic: job changes, partner problems, questions about where they live, and how people in their family are doing. The most exciting new trend I see is people wanting to find out how they can get this information for themselves. They want to know how they can sidle up to spirit and become psychic. The answer is: You are already psychic. It's just a matter of cutting some cords and peeling away some layers to reach it. Consider your own guides and me as your psychic personal trainers. For you to get results, we can't do the exercising for you; you have to do it yourself.

This is a journey of opening yourself up to your true calling, that of a psychic housewife. It's about revealing the woman and divine goddess you really are. Accomplishing that requires a tremendous commitment to self-care, self-trust, intuitive living, feeling your feelings, and an ongoing releasing of and allowing our children to experience their own highest good. There's no question our children can play a key role in our spiritual journey. They are also well taken care of when it comes to their own journeys.

One day I looked at all three of my kids (ages twelve, ten, and four) and said, "Kids, you can't get to God through me!" Three pairs of big blue eyes looked blankly back at me. But then a few minutes later, my ten-year-old son said, "Well, that's not a good idea anyway, is it? Don't you have to be with God yourself?"

Bingo! We have a winner in bedroom number one! That's the point, isn't it? No one can go to God for you; you have to make your own connection.

You and I are only the mothers in this scenario. We teach by the example of how we live our lives. If you are a real-life example of a woman who is hooked up directly to her own divine source, then you have true power.

If you want to fuel your life force, settle down first. If ladies with class drink from the glass, then ladies with sensation do meditation. In an ironic twist of events, quiet meditation actually fires up your energy, clarity, wit, and wisdom. Don't leave home without doing it. This is not a book intended to help you hook up with me and what I do. This is a book to help you hook up to your true self, your higher self, and God/Goddess energy.

In a nutshell, I'll give you some tips and thoughts about nature, nurture, letting go and letting God, living an inspired life, and getting the rest you need and the love you deserve. The more I learn in these areas, the more I know I don't know. In practicing these ideas in my life, however, the level of clarity, authenticity, love, and humor has gone off the charts. I've watched my children lead me and allow me to grow. My love for my husband has only blossomed.

I've also beaten my head against a few walls. My ego and I love to rush timing and force an outcome. That only causes me to throw a tantrum, which does not get results. Well, on rare occasions, screaming at the universe actually breaks things loose. The guides get sick of my high-pitched screaming and actually get me what I want a little earlier than planned. Mostly, however, I find myself feeling sidelined, waiting for divine timing. That too is part of this journey, learning to trust our circumstances. I've learned that God does have a plan and it is almost 100 percent not in alignment with my desired timing or perceived outcome. And it is usually 100 percent better than what I thought.

As my dear friend Helen Michaels likes to say, "The spiritual journey is a control freak's nightmare."

Since you are reading this book, I'm betting something really wild wants in right now. It is a feminine energy that allows your intuition to flourish. It leaves a mark on your heart and will never let you be the same. If you have the ability to see energy, this energy appears pink. My guides playfully tell me, "Pink doesn't stink and it is a link."

The contents of this book came from my life experiences, guidance from the angels, and many of my students (the women and some men who did in my classes the exercises included in this book). When I say students, I don't think of them as my students as much as students of spirit. I believe I'm a facilitator; it's my job to direct you back to your guides and inner guidance. That said, I don't think the magic happens without the exercise work. It's alchemy at its best. Your willingness to do the exercises is a key to this magic formula. Spirit is the fuel. You becoming psychic is the amazing result.

Exercises + Willingness + Spirit = Your Psychic Ability

So let's unleash our inner psychic. At the end of each chapter are assignments designed to enhance your innate psychic abilities. I suggest you try to complete the assignments over a two-week period, but you can use these assignments in any way you think would be helpful. You may want to form a small group of psychic housewives and do the assignments together each week. For years, women have been gathering on my website (www.psychic housewives.com), talking about these concepts and what happens when they apply them to their lives. They chat about their energy protection work, their self-care, their kids, and their psychic experiences.

Knowing this stuff is one thing, living it is quite another. This is a journey of having an experience. In a sense, it is about doing this stuff from the neck down. In the book, you will learn about shifting energy without using intellectual effort. The exercises, ceremonies, and prayers in this book are designed to bring you back to your body and its natural knowing. The book is about embodying spirit.

A friend of mine had constant stomach trouble. She thought she was eating the wrong food, but couldn't figure it out. When she finally learned the notion of the stomach being a feeling center, she found it was her body's way of telling her it was uncomfortable with certain circumstances or locations. Another friend found herself crying almost uncontrollably when talking to several people in her life. After those conversations, those people left her life abruptly, either through death or because they had a falling-out. She learned that her tears were part of her psychic knowing. Her body's reaction told her what was to come, even when her conscious mind did not get it. This is your opportunity to learn your body's signals and accept them.

If you are spiritually hungry, buckle up and get ready to have some experiences. You really don't know what's going to happen when you sign up for the ride. Women in this book have courageously attempted to embody spirit and share those experiences. They didn't get there by just reading my ideas. They got there by following a few suggestions, mingling it with their own internal guidance, and having some big feelings and experiences.

It is possible to become fully psychic overnight. But without the exercises and some support, it's not likely. Start working on this material. If you go to my website (www.psychichousewives.com), you'll find ways to get support on your journey. You'll also see that you really are having experiences similar to those of others. Also you can find my videos on many of these topics on YouTube. My channel is listed under, you guessed it, "psychic housewife."

You don't need to leave the comfort of your living room to have this experience. But you do need to leave your internal comfort zone to move forward. Now go for it! God's got your back!

Getting Started

The truth is, as a mostly stay-at-home mom I barely have time to write this book, so you probably don't have much time to read it. Sure, J. K. Rowling penned a bestseller with a young child sleeping on her lap at a coffee shop. But she had one child. I have three. That's the excuse I give myself anyway. I've read my share of new age how-to books. I haven't read many written around laundry, dishes, and kids running through the house.

Before enlightenment, make dinner and carry laundry.

After enlightenment, make dinner and carry laundry.

And listen to spirit yammer at you.

We hear the inner promptings and we see the visions, however briefly they appear. But when we consciously go to work on accepting their validity, it speeds up the enlightenment train. We are on the right track to waking up to a multidimensional world.

The ideas, theories, and exercises in this book have come through me directly from my spirit guides and some dead people. I also had some very good psychic friends channel amazing guidance. I've applied most of the concepts to my own life, and so have many of my psychic students. Think of us as some of the cooks at Betty Crocker for psychic moms with psychic kids. We test out a few suggested recipes to see what happens in our lives. Spirit only makes suggestions, but you have to be willing to bake the cake to see if it works. I thank the women who've walked through my psychic housewives courses online. They tested the recipes in their own lives and brazenly shared their feelings and results with everyone in class.

Here's what we'll be pondering, learning about, and getting our own psychic information about in this book:

1. **Excelling at self-care (doesn't that make your stomach turn?).**

2. **Setting physical/spiritual boundaries with people we love and people who really bug us.**

I've watched the discipline of doing self-care and setting boundaries create magical result for hundreds of women who are friends, clients, and psychic students. One of my clients called years ago to tell me she was overweight and also dating a man who wasn't very nice to her. My question for her was what was she doing to take care of herself. Her answer was "not much." The guides suggested she do more exercise, get some counseling, and take a good hard look at her boyfriend. I didn't hear from her for a long time. But when I did, the results were astounding. She'd dropped thirty pounds, dumped the guy, and done some counseling to understand some of her family issues. She'd also distanced herself from certain family members living in the same city, because she was tired of their constant criticism. She was very satisfied with her new way of life. She told me that launching into her self-care after our psychic reading made all the difference.

3. **Removing energy plants (that seem like innocent gifts at the time).**

4. **Clearing our homes and office spaces.**

A dear friend of mine was well along on her psychic journey when she realized she felt bogged down in her home. The energy inside her house felt thick and some-what unwelcoming. I offered to check in with her angels. She had been part of a professional women's group that she later left because she felt the leaders were very con-trolling of the members. It turned out during the reading that she still had many items in the house that members of the group had given to her. They came in as gifts and she had stuffed them away in closets and drawers. As we talked, she began to remember them and who gave them to her, and realized that she didn't want them in her home. After the reading, she went on a search-and-destroy mission. She collected all the items and threw them away. Then she did something equally important; she opened the windows and burned sage throughout the house. She says her home has felt homier ever since.

Items hold energy. Often they have the energy of the person who bought them or made them. If those people are not an energetic match for you, then neither is their stuff, even if it's a gift. Additionally, every time you remove old gifts from your house, you are moving around energy. That is why it is important to clear your home by burning sage after you remove items. We will cover the idea of clearing your space in detail in this book.

5. **Learning to tell the difference between your own intuition, other sources of psychic information, and the yammering of the ego.**

It can get confusing. Most of us are getting signals from our inner knowing, our bodies, outside people and ener-gies, and sometimes from a place itself.

Listening to your very insistent intuition can take

practice, but also delivers results. There are extreme and subtle examples of this. That's one reason a ticket for the Titanic is auctioned off for so much money. Someone listened to their intuition and didn't board a sinking ship. That's what I call a ticket to ride. In my practice, I've heard hair-raising stories from people who had a feeling about something and, in a single moment, made a life-altering decision. They either listened to their intuition or didn't. In this book, you'll learn to listen to your intuition and, I hope, come to understand what a lifesaver it can be.

People who are psychic can get very creeped out by historical buildings. A man I know who is psychic (but doesn't always admit it to himself or anyone else) went to Boston for a family vacation. He kept feeling the presence of ghosts, as though he were walking with soldiers from the Revolutionary War. Later, he relayed the story and I confirmed for him that he was walking with those ghosts, but at the time it was scary and confusing for him.

6. Grounding our energy.

I have had numerous clients over the years who felt like they were always floating over their bodies, instead of being inside them. A woman who works in finance told me she constantly daydreamed and lost track of details at her business. We went to work on helping her ground herself in her body. We talked about her eating more beef, spending more time outdoors, and setting a very grounding crystal called tourmaline on her desk. It worked. She came back to her body. Soon after, she left her job for one that suited her better and started having more fun in her body, getting massages and pedicures and eating delicious food. We came here to embody spirit. In this book, you'll learn concrete tools to use to be in your body and learn to access its psychic knowing.

7. **Allowing loved ones to get help from their own team of angels and friends and allowing them (especially children and partners) to experience their feelings about challenges and successes.**

I know a mother who finally decided to let go of her son. He was a young adult who had been struggling again and again to get sober. She constantly jumped in to rescue him. After years of struggling, she finally let go. That year he crashed. He lost his job, lived in a dumpy apartment, and drank himself into a stupor. It was incredibly painful for his mother. But she found support for herself so she could witness his journey rather than get involved personally in it. Later that year, her son joined Alcoholics Anonymous. He's now been sober for two years. She feels it took her letting go and letting God for her son to have the freedom to get sober.

Whether we have young children or teens, we can be tempted to take their journey for them. We can also do this with adults in our lives. In this book, you will learn to ask for guidance as to the best course of action for your kids and others in your life. Sometimes it's only after we let go that the miracles can happen. We see for ourselves that our children truly are taken care of by God and that we are simply their stewards.

An imperative part of the spiritual journey, the explosive jumping-off point, occurs when we engage in self-care and set firm boundaries with others. Your ability to be of service to others increases as you follow a plan of intuitive living and learn to say no first and foremost. It's time to redefine helpfulness to others, and learn how to help ourselves. As you move through these concepts, keep in mind that practice makes perfect. If you test-drive these notions in your world, I think you'll be pleased with the results.

A word of warning: The results will not be what you expect. They'll be far bigger than you can imagine. And some of what you're guided to do will likely scare you, make you mad, or call forth tears. But there's much joy waiting on the other side of a dance with heaven. Let's get started.

Psychic Laundry List

In this laundry list, you'll explore what psychic ability means to you and what psychic information is coming in for you right now.

1. Journal assignment: Reviewing your life, do you remember times you felt a strong inner guidance or intuition?

    A. Recall times when you followed your inner guidance or urging. What was the result?

    B. Do you recall any times when you felt inner guidance and did not follow this inner voice?

    C. How does your inner guidance manifest in your experience? Do you see pictures, have thoughts that feel like they are coming from a deep place within, just have a "knowing" about something? Journal about how your inner guidance shows up in your life.

2. What are some of your thoughts and feelings about the word "psychic"?

    A. What are your positive beliefs about being psychic?

    B. What are some of your negative beliefs? Journal about both the positives and the negatives.

3. Close your eyes and sit quietly for a few minutes. Notice your breath going in and out. Just be. Try this a few times a day. At the end of these few minutes, ask to be open to divine guidance. Or use any kind of terminology you feel might help open you up a little bit. Ask for inner wisdom, for your higher self to come in, or to be open to communication from your spiritual guides. Then just let it go for now.

✝✝Chapter 2✝✝
Self-Care, Boundaries, and Release

Now that you've spent some time remembering some psychic experiences and getting a taste for some psychic guidance, it's time to clear the air. It is imperative to give yourself a lot of safe space. When you're learning to work in the energetic realms, it's important to have a clear practice space to do it. In driver's education, you first get to simulate driving. You don't sit at a wheel and a real car comes into the room toward you. You have a safe space to practice. You watch a video and pretend like you're driving, but there's no real threat in the room. That's what we're doing in this chapter. We're creating a safe space for you to practice your psychic skills. We're also going to get you some more time and space to do it, so you can get your psychic driver's training license.

OK, let me guess . . . you have one, two, three or more children. Looking back at your mother, she was always giving, giving, giving. At least that's the story she tells. Despite all of her hard efforts, you found yourself feeling empty as an adult. Why? A dry well can't quench your thirst. If a mom doesn't protect her own energy, how in the hell can she take care of yours? She can't. And now that you're a mom, it is time to give it up, girl. Quit saving the world and save yourself first.

God and your guides don't want you to waste away in the desert of martyrdom. Think how irreverent we could be in our twenties and thirties. Today's moms hit their late thirties and early forties and they're whipped. We're chauffeurs, super volunteers, the household help, and part-time or full-time workers outside the home. Why? Because if we don't do it that way, our life and little Susie's life won't look PERFECT! And that would reflect poorly on us.

Here's the really, really bad news. Sacred feminine energy can be crazy! It truly could not care less about what outsiders think about the choices moms make. What am I talking about? I'm talking about saying no this year to the 205 volunteer commitments at school you've had for five years running. How about reducing Susie's activities to one single extracurricular activity per quarter? I'm suggesting you find time to meditate by leaving the kids to their own devices for twenty minutes a day. How about a daily routine of exercise to de-stress your body? How about a monthly massage or pedicure? Does it throw you if I suggest you have lots of sex with your partner?

Heather's Story

I am officially a self-care junkie! I've become more dedicated to listening to my body and taking care of myself. As women and mothers, we are natural caregivers and put everyone else's needs before our own. About six months ago, my guides talked to me about the amount of care, or lack thereof, I was giving myself. They told me I should change that right away.

My job, finances, and teenage daughter were and still are sources of stress. I was dedicated to being successful at work, and also trying to meet the needs of my daughter. During a psychic reading, my angels told me if I didn't start taking care of myself, everything else was going to begin to wear on me.

I wasted no time with that request. Everything they were saying made complete sense. I started taking care of myself and having fun! It felt so great. Time at the spa: Manicures, pedicures, and massages are all ways I enjoy taking care of myself. I know it's time for a trip to the spa when I'm feeling tired, stressed, and filled to the brim with too much to do. Yes, I put my "to do" list aside and take care of me. I have also found that when I take time for me, it makes my "to do" list much more tolerable!

As I write, I am feeling calm, peaceful, and content since I just finished receiving a full body massage. It has now become my monthly ritual!

No way! Can't do it! No way! Are your personal hounds of hell snapping and snarling? Don't worry, there is help. Many have heard of it, but few have dared to:

* Call a qualified counselor to help with a self-care plan.
* Join a support group such as Al-Anon. Al-Anon is a 12-step group designed to support people who have alcoholism in their family history. It has some powerful tools for help with codependency.
* Ask a girlfriend to help you reinforce your limits as a mom and volunteer.
* Take a meditation course.
* Actually sleep in some days and let Dad get the kids going.
* Sit down and feel your feelings.

In my case, it's taken an ungodly amount, or I should say a godly amount, of support from people and angels to get on this path. I went to a counselor who has a black belt in Al-Anon who asked me what I do to take care of myself. When I answered by listing off my family and volunteer commitments along with my career aspirations, he said, "No, Lorraine, I mean what do you do to take care of yourself emotionally?"

Uh, I was stumped. Today I'd be able to answer that question. But at that time, it took me an entire year of meeting with my counselor once a week even to begin to address it.

What are you willing to try on the journey of self-care? Here are a few suggestions for you to start out slowly. Try a few of these to see if you want to make them a habit:

* Say no this week to at least two requests for your time. Tell yourself you can always say yes later.

* Get rid of an item in your house that has been bothering you. Perhaps it feels like it has bad energy. Someone you no longer care for may have given it to you.

* If you're not already in therapy, make a call to find a counselor who will support you on your emotional journey.

* Take a nice luxurious bath with sea salt added to clear any negativity your body may have absorbed from others.

* Try to find a meditation class in your area that will support you in getting quiet and slowing down. (I know an amazing meditation teacher in St. Paul, Minnesota. I've sent many friends and clients who had trouble meditating to him, and most have successfully learned and continued to meditate. Check out www.psychichousewives.com for more information

about how to reach him. Believe me, it's worth the trip to Minnesota.)

* Take a walk in nature.
* Have really hot sex.
* Pray to be shown the most energy-efficient way to do all of the previous. Many women are living a daily life that miraculously includes raising children, doing meditation, going to nature, taking relaxing baths—and sometimes doing all of that on the same day.

When you put yourself first in the equation, the flood-gates of love open. It raises the river and lifts everyone with it. It truly creates miracles. But your ego will always beg to differ. It will make every attempt to control and manage your daily experience. The antidote is almost always more self-care, which equals self-love.

The biggest hurdle in doing something really nice for yourself often comes in the planning stages or when you're paying for it. That's when the ego sinks its teeth into your doubt, to stop you. Once you walk through that portion of it, though, the light floods in and you begin to feel giddy. It's also a powerful reminder that you are the boss. You are the adult who has to put the oxygen mask on first if the airplane is in trouble and your kids need help. When you do the self-care essentials, you beef up your motherhood and the kids also benefit. They also learn to leave you alone when you're headed to your room to meditate.

When I'm living these ideals, I feel the love. I still get tired and cranky, but less so when I'm doing self-care. Thank God, I finally understand that I'm not going for perfect. This is sloppy stuff! It leads you down the path of authenticity and to a more direct hookup with God. Women who sign up for this journey blossom. They trust their feelings and intuition more and more. They see bursts of synchronicity in their lives and experience increased contact by their spirit guides and deceased loved ones.

Take the suggestions in this chapter out for a spin and see what works. Are you getting any energetic results from saying no to "should" and yes to fun? Or is the whole experience making you cranky?

Letting Your Inner Garbage and Anger Up and Out

Since you're already taking the time to clear your space by dumping items that don't work for you, why not dump a few excess feelings as well? Remember, we're going for a clear safe place to practice your psychic abilities. There's no need for any extra obstacles. Feelings can be great barometers for where we're at and where we may be going. Feelings that have been built up over the years with no release, however, often create a backlog and haze that can keep us from seeing the truth of a situation. As part of our prep work, we're going to do some exercises that help us get current with God and our feelings.

My therapist was the first person in my life to tell me it was OK to get mad at God or your higher power. I was dumbfounded. I think it took me three more sessions for that bombshell to actually sink into my consciousness. I very tentatively got mad at God. Why had my mom left the family when I was so young? Why had I had a still-birth when I was nine months' pregnant? Why had I been so foolish about men and alcohol?

This was a start. Soon I would throw full-throttle temper tantrums. The further I go on the path of following spirit, the bigger my fits at God and the guides. They're not frequent, but I can guarantee at least once a year I get really mad and go into a full two-day rage. I've seen my four-year-old do it. Eventually, I get worn down and sometimes I give up and give in to his demands. Here's a secret—I've seen this work with my own guides and higher self. I throw a major fit, and the universe caves. Big feelings are powerful.

I got really mad about a huge credit card balance with a high rate (a choice I'd made earlier, while following divine guidance). The same week as my fit I got a call from the credit card company. They were dropping my interest rate to 2 percent and putting me on a five-year payoff plan. Somewhere, in the bowels of that bank, there was a lot of light reaching out to me. Frankly, just like my youngest son, I'm not sure I would have had the same results without an outrageous, extended tantrum. Releasing anger works.

The same goes for letting go of irritating people and situations in our lives. We hold the energy in our bodies. It wants out. It doesn't want to stay stuck. The guides have devised a few physical ceremonies or techniques for letting go and letting God.

Buy some old plates from a thrift store. Use permanent markers to write everything that's bothering you onto one or more plates. Then put the plates in a cardboard box or on the ground and smash them to smithereens with a hammer. Ooh, it's so satisfying and it releases so much energy into the universe. It also creates change. Try it, you'll like it. The more you enjoy the process and let go of the outcome, the more powerful the exercise is.

The other tried-and-true favorite of mine and many of my clients comes from the seraphim. These angels are from the realm of fire. The idea is you burn off what doesn't work anymore. It's simple. Write down everything that's bothering you on a piece of paper. Throw it into a pot and burn it. Go outside to do this if you can. Once the thoughts and feelings on paper turn to a crispy critter, pour water into the pot and dump it on the lawn.

Let the earth transform those worries. She is a master at it. The more real you get about your life, the more you release to your divine team, the more the negativity is transmuted. This is not about using effort to change things. This is in fact about backing off and letting God do for us what we can't do for ourselves. The process unleashes a powerful force. It is the beginning of allowing a force bigger than our ego selves to resolve matters.

Working with the elements is being truly magical. When you pull in the elements of water, fire, wind, and earth, you're really moving some energy around. If you can do the fire ceremony on a windy day without starting a fire in a field somewhere, then you've pulled in the element of wind.

There may be something you're called to do while out in nature that will release your feelings. Follow your gut on this one. Your inner knowing will pull you toward more clearing by interacting with rocks, trees, dirt, water, and the wind. Take time in nature as you get started on this journey. It is the most healing and clearing place you can be as you release your emotional baggage. This needs to be a light trip, so dump the extra suitcases.

Let's sum up the notion of self-care, boundaries, and releasing your feelings. When you are doing self-care, you're allowing and creating flow. It's interesting that the language of self-care is not passed on from mother to daughter. We learn how to care for others, how to be a nice girl and have manners. It becomes a model of self-sacrifice that follows us generation after generation. When you give until there's nothing left, there is no you left either. And I don't think that's what anyone in our immediate family wants. Our partners choose us because they want us around and the same goes for our children. On a soul level, they came to be with you as their parent. When you take care of you, you're ensuring you will be around in body, mind, and soul. Doing self-care, setting boundaries, and learning the word "no" are all matters of self-preservation and spiritual growth. When you shore up your energy, it ultimately makes you smarter about giving to others. Your relationships become equal energy exchanges, where you have enthusiasm to play with your husband and your kids. It sends your inner martyr packing.

Giving full expression to your feelings is also a life-affirming move. Then when you take the next step of releasing those thoughts and feelings to the universe and asking God and your angels to take them off your hands, you get tangible relief. If you are mad about some circumstances or people in your life that harmed you and you blame God, it's time to let God know. Releasing your feelings creates flow. Physically releasing your feelings to the universe makes it a reality to your ego. The action of smashing plates or burning papers with your feelings on them says, "I'm not staying stuck. I'm now handing off my anger, worry, and frustration to a bigger source. I am now invoking flow." There are very tangible ways to do your self-care. And those ways are fundamental to psychic ability. It is about showing your ego and the universe that you matter. When you genuinely love and care for yourself, it makes it so much easier to do that for others. It also creates a safe space to move ahead in the psychic housewives' handbook.

Psychic Laundry List

In this laundry list, you're practicing creating a safe space for yourself. You're also creating more room for your current feelings by acknowledging them and by releasing old ones.

1. Your first assignment is to throw out or burn something that was given to you by someone you intuitively know you don't like, respect, or trust.

2. Say no to at least one request you get this week, be it social or otherwise. I'm guessing you need a rest.

3. Do something that shows you really matter to yourself, whether it is a walk in the woods, a massage, extra baby-sitting for the kids, or a pedicure.

4. Buy a sage stick and burn it in your house with the windows and/or doors open. That's called clearing your space.

5. Ground yourself by sitting on the ground outside, eating beef, or catching a movie at the theatre.

6. Burn paper and/or break plates on which you've written your anxieties. Let the universe give you the relief you deserve.

✦✦Chapter 3✦✦

God as Driving Instructor, Helpful Passengers, and Beginning the Road Trip

OK, we're taking this driver's learning permit analogy one step further. You're now going to take your psychic ability learner's permit, get into your car, and practice your skills. Only in this case, you'll have a bunch of life-lines. God is your copilot and will be sitting in the front passenger's seat. If you're a soccer mom, you're probably used to loading lots of people into your car and playing chauffeur. Imagine you're driving a limo or a bus so you can also take as many family members, friends, and spirit guides as you like along with you. You'll be looking for road signs to show you the way. Allow yourself to make mistakes, which may include a few fender benders.

So how's it going? Were you able to say no? Clear the house? Do something to take care of yourself? I can see some of you—your heads are spinning. Your ego/brain is a little concerned. Don't worry, your higher self and guides are standing by to assist. This is breakthrough material. This is about cocreating with your soul to have a full, rich, satisfying, fun, and free lifestyle. Really, the guides mean it. You get to have all of that!

OK, I really don't like rules—suggestions maybe, but never rules. There is one fundamental truth about psychic ability, though. The platform is meditation. There are plenty of reasons to resist meditation. For starters, it's the beginning of the end of that feeling of separation from God and your higher self. While we wait for the true divine hookup, there are a lot of people and institutions willing to be a substitute for God. And that isn't a good thing. Conversely, there are plenty of people who avoid a direct connection with the divine and substitute priests, sponsors, psychics, and spouses for a higher power. I fondly call this latter group sheep. And I say it with empathy, because I've been in the flock. I've got some bad news: Divine is coming to get you. Like they say in my favorite line from the movie *When a Stranger Calls,* "We've traced the call and it's coming from inside the house!" If you have been drawn to spiritual books and videos, it is a good bet you are ready to go directly to divine. Even if you are struggling with believing in and seeing your angels, they continue to see and believe in you.

Eight years ago, a kind man in St. Paul, Minnesota, taught me to meditate. He told our class that teaching meditation is an oral tradition. That's why he believes reading how-to books on the topic doesn't always work. At the time I took the class, I was a workaholic reporter and a mother of two young children; I wore a pager, carried a cell phone, and was falling all over myself to volunteer in my 12-step group. A friend of mine who had been meditating regularly for fifteen years warned me meditation would change me forever. He was the one who invited me to go to the kind teacher to learn to meditate. I waited about seven years after his first invitation to accept. I'm no dummy. Who wants to bring in that much conscious contact with God?

Uh, yes, you could say that it changed things. Slowly but surely, things and people began to drop from my life. First it was the pager, then the job, the 12-step group program, and eventually my marriage. I got God and it was a local call, not long distance. I found a quiet place inside and let my intuition guide me. All the psychics that I know have a daily meditation practice. Many of my friends who are committed to divine guidance have committed themselves to a daily ritual of quiet. Praying for and listening to divine guidance are key components of having a direct line to divine.

Pray + Listen = Direct Line to Divine

The Seeming Insanity of Divine Direction

So, let's get back to the idea that you're driving a limo and you have your higher self/God as your copilot. Let's say God's telling you to drive down a dark alley. In your gut, you feel that may be the right choice, but your head is screaming not to do it. You decide to drive the limo there anyway, despite a lot of internal aggravation and fear. At the end of the dark alley, you turn right and find a specialty ice cream store that has your favorite flavor. You park the car, go inside, and learn from other customers that there was a huge traffic accident on the main street. If you'd gone that way, instead of taking the alley, you would have been stuck in traffic and missed the specialty ice cream store. Sometimes divine will direct us down a seemingly dark alley, which causes us to be extremely uncomfortable. But when we find our way out of it, we also discover it was a shortcut to a good thing. Experiment with following divine direction. Find out what happens if you follow the guidance. Do you get powerful results? Or do you feel tricked by the universe?

People who follow their intuition don't always feel it is easy or obvious. But the women I know who do it regularly swear by it as a method of having more personal freedom in their lives and having more adventures as well.

Sometimes I've snarled and gnashed my teeth over my angels' directions. Frankly, sometimes their input can be completely INSANE! Here are a few shining examples of guidance I received as I started my meditation practice and began listening to the messages:

Don't get a job even though you're broke.

Charge $40,000 on your credit card.

Leave Los Angeles.

Move back to Los Angeles.

Over the years I have learned that if I am confused about the message they're offering or trying to ignore it, it's usually repeated at least three different times from completely different sources. I can't fully explain to myself or anyone else why I started following my divine team's guidance seven years ago. It just felt like the right thing to do. I guess it just felt good to my gut. My body felt propelled toward a certain choice or action, especially when my brain was dead set against it. My ego is often confused about divine direction, but my heart is not. I've cried, laughed, yelled, and argued about many of my divine directives, but I know that the still small voice within is the one to listen to in times of confusion.

Many of the men and women (clients and friends) I've spoken with over my years of readings are searching for support to take action on their intuitive feelings. The world around them seems to tell them it is crazy to follow their dreams and desires. Sometimes acting on their intuition involves changing a job or quitting work altogether. Sometimes it means the call to a spiritual quest, such as building up their psychic abilities. When I'm doing the readings, looking from the outside in and listening to their guides yammering at me, everything they are being asked to do is actually a call to put more love and life force back into their lives. It's about not blocking the natural flow and it's also about letting God clear out the junk to make way for something better.

Helen's Story

I first awoke to a more conscious spiritual path back in 1982. With the birth of my daughter came the birth of my own spirit. It was a dark night of the soul and I eventually developed an understanding of communication with spirit especially through my art making and Julia Cameron's *Morning Pages*. I was guided to jump career tracks from graphic design to art therapy and ended up working for an experiential education program for adults experiencing a mental illness. I discovered that Spirit is particularly bold in communicating through clay.

Working with my intuition became a daily interaction. Building any sort of trust took me years, but when I finally went about it like a scientific experiment things speeded up. Spirit's best chance to commune with me was during my morning pages and art-making sessions . . . It was probably because that's a meditative state and my ego was more out of the way (although still very present). As I reflect back over my life and now have terms for our psychic communication styles, I see that I experienced clairsentience (clear feeling) and claircognizance (clear knowing) from early on in my life.

Quite frankly, my ego hated it because it heightened the possibility of looking "crazy." When you know things you shouldn't be able to know, well, that's hard to explain logically! The same is true for clairsentience, and all the psychic abilities for spirit communication. My ego just could not integrate it into the person it believed I needed to be for my well-being. It is so ironic that upon gaining access to all these psychic styles, I feel more "at home" than I ever did before.

After years of receiving personal energy work, I decided to take a "Light Body" course. It was the closest I had come to being able to admit my interest and desire to actively learn more of the "psychic skills."

The next phase of the deconstruction aspect of my personal reconstruction began. I became painfully aware that my relationship-building skills were firmly entrenched in a codependent style. Spirit was simply not going to allow me to continue in this way. A big period of all types of "losses" ensued. The loss of people through a direct choice of ending contact, death, and drifting apart began. I also lost my sense of identity, of how my ego knew who I was. Like a game of falling dominoes, chunks in all areas of my life fell down and away.

My ego could never have imagined living without many of these connections in my life. As my relationships melted away, I began to turn more toward Spirit for support and comfort. Meditation class turned out to be a perfect gateway for this new direction. It gave me the opportunity to learn how to be willing to open to conscious contact and actually show up to it twice a day, almost like a standing "date." This put me more directly in the driver's seat to pursue my own spiritual and psychic development.

Once I let go of explaining and trying to convince people of anything, doing what I needed to do for myself became a whole lot easier. By September, I was completely out of all my organizational entanglements and couldn't believe how light I felt. I was now living in a previously unimaginable state. My ego was in shock, but the sense of freedom I experienced was so grand that I didn't spend much time thinking about all that had happened.

In my case, everything about my life has changed since I put my ear to the rail of the Holy Grail. I decided to listen to the call of my spiritual quest. It's a journey toward a more feminine, feeling approach to life. It has become a lesson in allowing others to follow their path and allowing myself to let go of what I think I need to be happy. I've learned to hold on lightly to what I have in my life. It's taken some drastic measures by divine to get me to release my news career, my relentless style of guilt-ridden mothering, and my desire to live in a really, really big house.

During the writing of this book, we spent time living in our log home in the northern woods of California. We also spent time living in a tiny apartment where the two adults and three children in our family would come and go and sleep on air mattresses. The small living space put the squeeze on us. Finally, we moved into a house with three bedrooms and two thousand square feet in the Los Angeles area. I know it all built flexibility muscles. I have owned a home as big as six thousand square feet and have also lived out of a suitcase in an eight-hundred-square-foot apartment with my family. I'm finally learning that the old adage "You can't take it with you" can apply while you're still on Earth.

It's easier moving between the realms when you are light on your feet. Now more than ever, I truly see how little I need materially to have my life work. I know the bigger place is coming and our family does need more space, but not much.

Our place is packed full of love, feelings, creativity, and acceptance. It is partially the result of a crazy partnership I've made with divine; I constantly follow direct heavenly guidance. Here are some tips for hooking up with divine in a very personal way:

* Find a meditation practice (preferably taught in person).
* Meditate daily.
* Pray daily for the outcome of highest good.
* Pray for clear divine guidance from beings of highest consciousness.
* Journal about the answers you feel you've received.
* Follow the guidance and see what happens.
* Build a human team to support your intuitive journey.
* Allow your feelings to come up and out.
* Fasten your seat belt—it's a wild ride.

Sandy's Story

This is the story of a dream come true, or more accurately, a dream buried deeply and excavated with the stubborn and persistent help of divine guidance, which has finally come true. Only now do I see that dreams are like love. They grab your heart tightly, take your breath away, and radiate throughout your being, creating energy and joy.

I live in Sausalito, California. From my two-bedroom apartment, I have a view of the San Francisco Bay, from Angel's Island past the Bay Bridge to the local marina. It's warm and the sky is cloudless. All of which is only a big deal because never in my wildest imagination as a child of the Midwest did I think I'd be living here.

My youngest child graduated from high school three years ago and went off to college. Minneapolis had lost energy for me long before; I'd been biding my time, waiting for him to leave in order to leave myself. I fully expected to sell my house and move somewhere that fall. But the somewhere that I'd been looking for, the lover, client, or new business idea that would take me away, had not shown itself yet. Then my daughter begged me to stay just through Christmas; it would be her last Christmas home while she was finishing college. So stay I did. But not before getting a Realtor's estimate on the house.

After thirty years of living and working in Minneapolis, all the magic it had held earlier was gone. I was comfortable but not happy. I'd ceased to have energy for new activities and new people there. I'd been talking about leaving, but no one really thought I would.

I fell in love with San Francisco when I visited a

39

college friend there in the mid-1970s. On that first visit, we drove through Sausalito, even had the Sunday champagne brunch at the Alta Mira. And though the city captured my heart and imagination, it was Sausalito, with its European charm, hillside homes, steep windy roads, bay vista, and long stretch of shoreline with luxury shops and restaurants, that seemed the fairy tale place.

Last year I consulted Lorraine for help with reenergizing the work I'd become so bored with. The message was simple and straightforward: "They keep saying your answers are at the ocean." It was not what I'd asked for. There was no help with work. By this time, I'd decided a move was too much for me and said so. But another visit was doable. Lorraine left me with a poignant question: "What are you willing to do for your soul?"

I was journaling at my favorite coffee shop and asked the question about what I'd be willing to do for my soul. The answer included "not working." I wondered, if I was willing to walk away from a comfortable consulting practice, what would the universe do to support me? Would the universe help me move, given the condition of the real estate market and problems I'd witnessed firsthand with a friend who'd struggled for a couple years to sell her home? I figured, if my house would sell easily, for the price I wanted, I'd be free to move. I guess I was challenging divine a bit, for more obvious help. So without saying much to anyone, I spent the summer preparing my house to be sold. If it sold, then I'd figure out where to go.

The house sold in two days. Now, completely free of the financial obligation of property, whimsically I decided to check out the San Francisco Bay Area and the Monterey Peninsula for a rental in which I would be comfortable, where my kids and friends could visit, that I could afford. I told myself and others, that if it was not doable financially, I'd go to Seattle where I have a close friend. I started in Sausalito. On the second day, the perfect flat presented itself. I didn't need to look any further. I knew that Sausalito would be my next home.

It's only now that I am here that I am aware of how it is a dream come true. And that it took the insistence of my guides to show me the way.

Your Earthly Support Team

So you're driving the limo and you've loaded up the back with your human support team. Who's in there with you? Is it your spouse, your kids, your friends, or members of a support group? Are they trying to back-seat drive or are they yelling their support for the choices you are making with God as your driving instructor? It can be common to feel alone on this path when you start exploring your psychic ability. With busy spouses and friends who are often buried in their kids' commitments, it can be a challenge to follow your intuition or find someone to talk to about your spiritual journey.

The journey to enlightenment can go quickly when you have kids. There are two or three mini Buddhas running around your house to pass along their mastery of living in the moment. Your family and close friends are your entourage. Christ had his disciples and you have your partner, kids, and girlfriends. If your husband's pulling down the big bucks, or an average amount of bucks, he's supporting you by creating more time for you to follow spirit. He's also providing more time for your kids to be with Mom. He may not completely understand your new curiosity about psychic ability, but if he's working hard and allowing you free time to explore it, he is supporting you on an energetic level.

Your kids will work with you by pressing all of your buttons, saying amazing things that seem to be straight from God, and being pure life force. They are incredible examples of living in the flow and having a direct connection to divine. Years ago, I was nervous about a presentation I was doing in Minneapolis. I told my son Nathan who was only three at the time and he quietly said, "You don't need to worry, Mommy. God will be there and all will be well."

I felt it was from divine through Nathan to me. All three of my children have said beautiful and amazing words of grace to me over the years. I know they're on my team.

My husband has generously supported me for a lot of my journey. He was with me when my psychic abilities came flying in. He knew me before that when we were just coworkers. I was a no-nonsense reporter. He now knows me as a softer, much more emotional, psychic woman, mom, and lover. Without all four of these people in my life, I really don't know how I'd have made it these last many years. They are all truly earth angels.

Another form of support is, of course, friendship. Girlfriends can prop you up in the most amazing ways. They listen unconditionally, hug you when you cry, and laugh with you at the absurdities of life. If you need to load up the limo with support, be sure to bring along some women friends. Be on the look out for gals who have integrity beyond reproach, an amazing capacity for love and support, and are seen laughing a lot.

Mentors and healers can also offer invaluable experience, teachings, and energy work. Knowing someone who's been on an intuitive path for a while can help teach you how to avoid certain pitfalls. In addition, going to a trusted energy practitioner can really smooth out some of the kinks in your body and journey.

The Internet can be a wonderful way to connect with people who are exploring their psychic abilities. Besides my psychic housewives chat group, there are others out there on the Web discussing spiritual topics. There are also many resources at local new age bookstores and healing centers. Finding a class or meditation group with like-minded people is a good way to tap into some support.

The idea of being alone is a version of hell. It's the illusion of separateness. But it's exactly that, an illusion. Ask the universe to assemble and screen an A-team to support you on your courageous journey of being a spiritual being in a human existence. You'll probably find your team is a mix of family, old friends, new acquaintances, and maybe a few professionals, such as a counselor or an energy healer. The biggest actors, rock stars, athletes, and religious leaders in the world have entourages. Life's a trip, but not one to be taken alone. Load up the limo with your entourage. This can be a party, though it's not always fun. This team needs to be able to hang with you through the ups and downs of the journey. They won't be going through all the same experiences as you, but they will be witnessing many of them. It's lovely to have great friends on a good road trip.

Your Divine Support Team

Speaking of road trips, one time I was driving my big

SUV and I suddenly saw my guides with me. There were a bunch of guys smoking pipes. On the seat next to me was an elf. He had very short legs and pointy shoes. I can't believe I'm writing this! But honestly, I saw it plain as day. As you work your way through your divine team, you'll learn that some of the members can be pretty silly. The hallmark of a great team is a lot of humor and visual cues about who they are. You may see them do music videos or they may send you funny signs. Watch them trip you up when you are hell-bent on doing things your ego's way. Have you been getting the feeling you want to do something very specific? Has someone psychic suggested a certain course of action? Has a recent song, video, or book crossed your path that seems to send a message directly to your heart? Your angels, guides, and higher self have many ways of getting your attention.

Do you wonder who's talking to you and if you should be listening? It's your divine right to ask questions about your heavenly support team and ask them to prove their integrity and credentials.

Get names. Get images. Get specifics. Get their intentions. This is an opportunity for you to practice self-authority. Your guides should be entities that you like, respect, and trust. It's important that their guidance lines up with a gut knowing about your next steps. Of course, some of the tasks your soul has signed up to undertake may bring tears or anger. But the guidance should line up with an inner knowing about which next step to take. If you're hearing a message that seems to be negative or lacking love and humor, chances are you're hearing from low-level entities. Set your intention to only hear guidance from beings of highest consciousness, end of story.

Now, will some nasty entities cross your path? They probably will. It's a complex multidimensional world. But you can notice them and move along. In the case of your spiritual advisors, it's best when they are based in integrity and divine light.

It's also entirely possible that you will be guided by a heavenly team member to do something that doesn't feel right to your gut. Ask for more explanation from your higher self, a trusted psychic, or a good counselor. It's completely OK if you decide not to pursue a divinely suggested course of action. Sometimes team members can be a bit off the mark or they may be testing your self-authority. Just as you would do with a human team member offering advice, do a gut check to see if what your divine guide is suggesting is a fit with your inner knowing.

Feel your way through your team and write down your memories of being helped by divine and what form it took. Some of us have felt an affinity for fairies, dragons, unicorns, and other magical creatures. There are often crystal allies that call your name. Or perhaps wild animals have appeared to you in nature, in your dreams, or in divination cards. Members of your heavenly support team will take on just about any form you can imagine to get a message to you or just to show you their support. As an example, I felt bad yesterday so I stayed home from work. I almost never call in sick to work, but I did it. Then I felt like it was important to keep transferring this book from my notepad to the computer. I was sitting at the computer feeling guilty and a song from the 1990s came on the Internet radio that I often listen to when I'm feeling bad. The chorus is "Rock-a-bye, everything's gonna be all right." Later in the afternoon I checked the mail and there was a utility refund check for the exact amount of money I would have made at work that day. I knew it was my higher self and my guides telling me I'd made the right choice.

If you doubt there is support, ask the universe to be specific and give you signs and indicators about your team. Who are the members? How do they show themselves? What are they telling you?

Let's pretend for a moment that you're an exquisite Tiffany lamp about to plug in to the divine electric socket. Your only job is to be the lamp and trust that the electricity will be there and someone will change the light bulb when needed. The biggest hurdle in the journey is to trust your soul and your team, and drop the effort. You don't have to work harder; you just have to throw your light. Get to know your divine maintenance team, then you can relax more and enjoy the exquisite light in the world you are meant to be!

Signs

It's hard to drive, if you don't pay attention to the road signs. If you're steering the limo, you're getting feedback from your divine copilot, and you've got support from the back, then the next simple step is to keep your eyes on the road. Divine is everywhere and always willing to give you a hint about where to turn, when to stop, and most certainly when to slow down. If you keep looking at the clock and seeing repeating numbers such as 11:11 or 4:44, it may be your angels just saying hello. They may also be asking you to look up the symbol of a certain number. For example, one is complete and four is heavenly. Repeated images, song lyrics, or words are also a sure sign you're being shown a sign. If you find yourself thinking, "I can't believe I'm seeing this again," chances are your guides are trying to get your attention.

I've heard stories over and over again about clients and friends who know they are rushing through their lives. About that time, they get pulled over for speeding. Don't kid yourself, it's the angels' way of saying they're policing those of us who just can't slow down and make time for quietly listening to our guides.

When using my angel card deck, I often get the "sign" card. I've had some humdinger signs in my time. Sometimes I only recognized them later. On Saturday, I pulled a dragonfly card, then later one landed on my leg as I floated down the river. Dragonfly is about believing in yourself and your divine abilities. The same week, I was worried about money, posted a blog (#169), and someone sent me a message saying that the number 169 means don't worry about money. In Los Angeles, I often see posters about fairies. The latest was when I went to Disneyland. A photographer there lined my family up on Main Street and told us to hold out our hands and look surprised. Well, they put Tinker Bell in our hands, thanks to computer technology. It was the same week fairy images seemed to be everywhere I looked and I knew the photo was another affirmation that the fairies were saying hello.

One woman I know frequently sees feathers falling out of nowhere. The symbolism there can mean a feather from an angel's wing. Another sees rubber bands everywhere on the ground and in very unlikely places. They remind her of angels' halos. For myself, I constantly find small colorful rubber balls in strange places. It reminds me of the colorful personalities of many of my guides. Just this week, I went into a clothing store and literally stepped on a two-inch thick rubber ball. I put it in my car cup holder as a reminder that my team is with me.

What are the recurring signs the universe provides you? Whether it's reassurance or a warning, what is it that's caught your attention? Opening up to seeing signs from your guides means you are accepting their help. Sometimes a sign can simply be a way for the guides to let you know they're with you and sometimes it's about directing your divine limo to the outcome of the highest good.

The Undoing

This next part of the journey is where the ride can get a bit dicey. Now that you've connected with your higher power (through meditation), acknowledged that divine direction can seem insane, and assembled your team of humans and angelic guides, it's time to release control of the journey. Now you're going to swap seats with God or your higher self. God's taking the wheel and you're moving to the passenger seat. Have you ever seen those intense movies where someone's trapped in the passenger seat with a crazy driver? Well, that's what we're talking about here. This is the ultimate act of faith. You've only just received your own psychic driver's license, and you're suddenly being asked to hand the wheel over to divine.

Wait a minute, wait a minute, you might protest. Why should I hand the keys over to this seeming nut job? Well, first of all, you are actually turning the keys over to yourself, your higher self. And second, this aspect of your self has an out-of-this-world global positioning satellite system. Your God aspect sees things from a higher, longer-term view. And she knows a lot of shortcuts that may end up being a lot of fun. This driver doesn't always stay on the main road, can alternate between speeds of five miles per hour and 105 miles per hour, and very rarely explains where the limo is eventually going to land. The limo may shape-shift into a station wagon or a convertible, your support team may change, and some of your luggage in the trunk may bounce out and be lost forever. Allowing divine to take the wheel can mean letting go of a lot of what you think you need. But it can also mean a very exciting ride.

Most of what I've learned on this journey began on surface streets and took a quick trip through a tunnel to the underworld, into what felt like hell or death energy. Isn't that enticing? Don't I make a great recruiter for the divine journey? But the truth is, the more you go for God, the more quickly every place you feel separate from divine is revealed. That's when the big feelings of shame, anger, sadness, and fear emerge. It's a version of living in hell. The feelings of abandonment, confusion, and betrayal indicate the places where you are not feeling one with God.

You will find everything about your life shifting as you set your intentions to hook up with divine. Friends come and go, and the way you see people and the world changes. Your career aspirations leave or come into focus and everyday chores and responsibilities can overwhelm you. Why? Because you're going back to your true form, which is multidimensional. A standard 3-D container can't hold the big divine energy. That's why you'll find yourself bursting into tears with what seems to be little provocation. You'll choose to rest rather than clean, and you'll crave sweet or fatty food without warning. Your body, your family, and your dwelling are taking the trip with you. All may contract and then expand at various stages of the journey. Absolute and total confusion is a sure sign your higher self and body are riding in the limo. Sometimes the ego wants to stay back at the curb. Reluctantly, it will climb into the car, but not without a fight.

Spirit may woo you with the mystique of psychic ability. It is a trick. When I first became fully psychic at the age of thirty-nine, it knocked me out. I thought my life would change dramatically, that I would have amazing career opportunities and have all the answers about my own life. The gift of seeing brought many more questions than answers and seemed to shut out my ability to make a living in the working world. I did make some money doing readings at home and was grateful for that, but my income dropped from eighty thousand a year to about eight thousand a year. I gained weight, my face aged, and I felt inexplicably tired. True, during that time I had a baby at age forty and was also raising my two other young children, but that didn't completely explain the changes going on for me.

Now, as I write this, things are turning around. My kids are in school or day care. I've joined a gym, have a part-time job, and have hired a housekeeper. I still get knocked out during the full moon, get overwhelmed at malls by all the people, eat food that's bad for me sometimes, feel exhausted, and cry at unexpected times. I'm not going to sugarcoat it. If you're on the path to psychic living, things are going to change rapidly. The biggest change will be in you and how you relate to the world.

Our physical and spiritual support teams get us through the tough times and all the changes. Of course there are a million miracles, coincidences, and blessings that counterbalance all the tough stuff on the spiritual path. But it's important to be realistic and expect some rough terrain.

Psychic housewives, be warned!

As you get more accustomed to psychic living, you realize your head sometimes feels like it is filled with cotton. You can feel confused and dazed, especially at times when you're supposed to be making big choices. That is your guides' way of unplugging your brain so your intuition can do its best work. It may not feel pleasant when it happens, but it can often produce some amazing results. It's the universe's way of stopping your forward motion, before you do something really stupid. Time and time again, I've found myself in the right place at the right time after I've given up trying to "figure out" the situation or the best course of action.

Here's what I learned at the Living Desert in Palm Desert, California, at the Butterflies Alive exhibit. When a caterpillar forms a chrysalis, it forms it on the inside. So the caterpillar's head falls off in the process (no longer needed for eating leaves) and the butterfly bursts out of its former body. I looked at Tammy, the woman explaining all this, and said, "Whoa, I can relate to that right now!"

Since you are agreeing to lose your mind to find the divine, now is probably a good time to get a designated driver. So how do you locate your divine copilot? You find her by consciously opening up the channels of communication. You then build your human and heavenly team and invite them to load up in your car for your trip.

While you're driving, you keep your eyes on the road, watch for signs, and listen to your copilot who's in the passenger seat next to you. Then when you feel ready, you hand the wheel over to a seemingly crazy divine driver who knows more shortcuts than your ego/mind does. Finally you buckle up and dare to see where the driver and the road lead you.

The first step to connecting with divine is finding a form of meditation that suits you. Ask your heavenly helpers to find a method that's right for you, then relax and know it is coming. Getting quiet and allowing silence is the baby step to hooking up with divine in a conscious way. You're already a divine being. Meditation brings in a more tangible knowing of that truth. It also creates a pipeline coming and going from source to you. Of course, we have our inner divine, but in the beginning, we often find the structure and guidance in a way that seems to be coming from the outside. Sometimes these sources are operating at a different vibration, which makes them difficult to see or hear. Meditation changes our vibration and allows us to receive the messages. We're in a better place to ask who our divine team is. As we are able to see and hear them, we build a more conscious connection with them. A regular meditation practice gives our ego/brain a way to connect to something that has seemed intangible. We are filled with a feeling of being supported and loved by our angels. Psychic ability moves from being a concept to an experience we believe.

Our increasing awareness allows us to take a good look at our human entourage and support system. We are physical bodies who need other people. Getting and giving support are fundamental components of our daily lives and our spiritual journeys. Becoming acutely aware of who is on your team and the role they play in your daily life is a fundamental aspect to your psychic journey. Asking for help from family, friends, a sponsor, or a counselor can feel embarrassing or humbling, but it is key to growing psychically and emotionally.

Having our heavenly and human teams in place creates a support network for the undoing that can come with growing psychic abilities. When your perspective and circumstances are changing rapidly, you need all the help you can get. There will be a lot of give and take in these times. Your friends and family will also be experiencing their own changes, so you can support each other through it all. Your divine team will support you. And at times your divine team may ask you to help someone. Because you're tapping into your intuition more, spirit will send you to be of service.

Asking for and receiving support is imperative. So is allowing the falling away of the old. Spirit will be asking you to stay current. That means being an energetic match with people and circumstances in your life. When something no longer feels right, chances are it isn't. The universal energies will often initiate some of the changes for you, however, like having you fired from a job, having your boyfriend break up with you, or causing you to get sick so you slow down. Conversely, your higher self and guides will often cause change by making job and relationship opportunities happen quickly. Your only real job is to stay in communication with divine, ask for and receive support, and do regular self-care.

Psychic Laundry List

This chapter's exercises are all about preparing for an adventurous road trip with God.

1. Try finding a meditation practice that works for you. The quiet is essential to listening to your higher self and guides. This, again, is not to be turned into a "should." Just invite in meditation. For you it may include a walk in the woods, yoga, or your simple quiet time alone. As the guides say frequently during readings that I do, "This is your life. It isn't a dress rehearsal." If you, like many, are feeling the push to truly connect with your soul and spirit guides, be willing to lay the foundation.

2. In meditation, ask who your main guides are. You may see just one; you may see more than that. I know all of you have at least a main guide working with you at all times. Ask them to show you or tell you something about themselves. Also, ask them to tell you or show you a joke about you or your current life. And finally ask them to make contact with you in the physical world. Write down some of the signs you have seen lately. Some examples from my clients include seeing rubber bands (representing halos), feather floating down (symbolizing angel wings), and dimes (meaning that life can turn on a dime). Remember, spirit is often gentle and silly. If your intuition tells you it's contact and it makes you smile, it's a divine touch. And take your time with this exercise. If it ends up being frustrating, just let it go. Ooh, this is going to be SO FUN!

3. Who's on your earthly support team? Make a list of who's in your inner circle. Do you like who's there or do you need more help? Ask your heavenly team for assistance on the ground, so that you have the entourage you need to support your spiritual growth.

4. Journal assignment: What are you willing to do for your soul?

✦Chapter 4✦
Wake Up, Sleepyhead!
It's Time to Really See

This is the chapter where you find out seeing is believing. Sometimes just being willing to see what you intuitively know is out there can be a huge breakthrough for your psychic ability. When you fall asleep at the wheel, you have a higher likelihood of crashing. Slam a double espresso and let's take a look at you, your life, and who's lurking in the shadows. Let's also find out how truly wonderful and interesting your spouse and children are. You'll step out of your preconceived notions into the present moment.

Ghosts

If it took a ghost to get you to this book, then bravo! Chances are good that your child saw it first. They do that and suddenly Mommy starts the journey down spiritual lane, trying to see and fix the ghost problem. If you have a haunting, here's the talk I'd give you if you called me. Sometimes families decide the ghosts are cute and funny. The ghosts aren't bothering us that much, so who cares? Well, let's say you and your child sense that the ghost is an older woman who's cranky. She shows herself to the kids and makes noise at night. Let me ask you this, if the woman were there in the flesh, would you want her living with your family? Honestly, it's just not that cute to have a perfect stranger rattling around the house talking to your kids. As the woman of the house, it is not only your right, but also your obligation to kick her behind out of there.

Sure, you could call a ghostbuster, or you can keep reading and I'll offer a few tips to do it yourself. Have you ever stayed in someone's home a little too long? Mark Twain said fish and visitors smell after three days. What's my point? The ghost may seem to have the power to make your life unpleasant and to stick around. But believe me, a really angry mother who's also a burned-out hostess can make it very unpleasant for an unwanted guest. If you really decide you're fed up, grab some spiritual tools and get going.

The first order of business is to get your family on board. Everyone (the kids, husband, and the family dog) has to agree it's time for the ghost to go. Then say a prayer together that the ghost moves on to a better realm and that your family gets assistance with divine protection. The family that prays together, stays together, and dumps the ghost. Next, when the house is empty, call the ghost to you, ask what she wants, listen patiently, and then kindly tell her she has to leave. Whether you have heard from the ghost yourself, just know it's around, or are onto it because your child tells you about it, it is still up to you to shoo it away. It's important to remind the ghost that no one can get to God or to heaven through another person, family, or someone's house. It's a solo journey to get the hookup. And it's not OK for a lost soul to look for a shortcut through your family.

Next, give the ghost last call: "You don't have to go home, but you can't stay here."

Invite them to go home to heaven (the light), but if they decide not to go there, tell them they can't stay at your place. Bye-bye! Next, open the windows, light a sage stick, and say a prayer giving thanks for a clear home. The end.

Now this is important: You and your family are not to give the ghost any more of your time, thoughts, or energy. Thinking about the ghost can and will draw it back to you. Just say no. There are better ways to play with spirit that are more fun. You don't need a haunting to connect with the other side—not when you're a psychic house-wife.

All of that being said, there are kindly spirits wandering around and close encounters with ghosts in places besides your home. Those can be fun and enlightening experiences. What I'm talking about here are the lost souls wandering the earth, landing at your place, and behaving badly. They get the boot.

On the energy continuum, there's light and dark and a lot in between. When ghosts figure out you can see or hear them, they want to be seen and heard. Who wouldn't, right? Their will does not supersede your own, however. You have a divine right to be safe and sound in your own home and out in the world. Sometimes you are challenged with ghosts and other forms of darkness as part of your own divine growth. I have psychically battled with sorcerers, ghosts, aliens—you name it. And you know what? I've always received the help and information I needed and the energetic support. I've also discovered that within me there's darkness looking for light.

And that's made me really smart about energy boundaries, reading dark energy, getting help, and self-care.

Some of you who've had ghost problems or dark-energy issues are emerging into a more powerful realm. You're doing great work! This is where the rubber meets the road and you will be challenged. You will have to be afraid, walk through it, and step into your strength and, more important, the protection of spirit (you will eventually discover that you and spirit are one and the same).

A year ago I was friends with a healer who was really dancing in the dark. She simply did not have enough self-authority in place to repel all the energy coming off clients and a certain area where she lived. I went to a gypsy/psychic at a street fair near my house in Los Angeles. (I'd never seen her before and haven't seen her since.) She pulled a tarot card that had beautiful baby angels holding swords. She told me I was very protected, but that my life path had been to have a lot of interference. Amen! She also said I needed to stay away from my healer friend for several months and that I, too, had darkness in and around me. Well, let me tell you, I was shocked. Me? Darkness? Then the universal truth dawned on me: What we need to heal is often reflected back to us by those around us. So I did some of my own clearing and work with darkness. I even asked for a dark-arts master (in spirit form) who was mostly a good guy, and I got one. He taught me a lot. I now realize you can take some of that dark energy and turn it on its head. But you can't do that from a place of fear. One of my specialties was reading darkness around people. Since doing this work with my darkness within, however, I don't get those kinds of people or clients coming around as much anymore.

And I almost never have ghosts around. My boundaries are in place.

So here's an exercise. Ask to see if you have darkness around you. See what shows. This might be damn scary, but know you're safe and protected. Next, ask to see what protection you have in place. Ask to see your team. Don't be surprised if you see no less than a hundred beings of light. You are walking in light, whether you know it or not.

Now visualize around you a fortress with lots of padding and mirrors hanging on the outer wall, so that whatever dark stuff is looking at you, it also sees itself. You're shining a mirror in its face. Get it? This is powerful stuff.

Imagine a beautiful pink spaceship beaming a love ray at any intruders, zapping them in a loving, but powerful way.

You can say, "I'm not a ghost host." You can also say, "I call on my guides of highest consciousness to clear my sacred circle and protect it and me." You can also post angels in all four corners of your house or apartment and workplace.

Look, you can't just do light all the time. When I was young, I asked my dad why I couldn't have ice cream every day. He said because I wouldn't appreciate it as much when I did have it. Well, you can have light every day. But see how much more you appreciate it when the dark rears its head? I used to take ghosts and darkness very seriously. Now, I often laugh them off. When you're serious, you're probably also afraid. When you're laughing, you're in the moment and powerful. Give those dudes a raspberry and let's move on.

Sorcerers and Wizards

Now we're going to look at things in black and white. Life is rarely so clear-cut. But for the purposes of seeing more clearly, take a look at yourself and the people in your life by using the following two categories.

Sorcerer: An Energy Vampire
Wizard: Has a Direct Hookup to God

Who doesn't want a freebie once in a while? I mean, my goodness, we're all working our behinds off to make a living, keeping up with housekeeping, and raising kids. We're working hard. Then along comes someone who feels the same way and who really understands energy and they make a free meal out of guess who? You! Here are signs of an energy vampire. They have a difficult time taking responsibility for themselves. They don't acknowledge or apologize when they have done something wrong. They rarely ask for help directly, but usually order you around or make passive-aggressive comments or hints. They drone on and on about themselves. They're outwardly focused (in critical ways) on people, their career, and their circumstances. They are rarely introspective and do not appreciate honest feedback from others. There is rarely an intention for real communication.

If you are someone with natural enthusiasm and a unique life force, are very creative, and communicate openly, watch out, the vampires are lurking. They can try to steal your love, your energy, your creativity, and your attention and they'll suck you dry. This is not an equal energy exchange. This is a date with Dracula. He looks good at first glance, but at night, out come the fangs. In the morning, you wake up with puncture wounds. Energy vampires of this world take many forms. They can look like perpetual victims, guilt-wielding committee chairs from the kid's school, or a friend who just won't stop talking about herself. Sound harsh? It is. It's harsh on you and your energy.

The more often you say no to these energy-suckers, the more you'll start to see. "No" is not a word energy vampires like to hear. It's a word, however, they like to say when you ask them for something authentic, such as asking for honesty, their time, listening, being noncompetitive, or making a commitment to your well-being. Look, there's nothing wrong with running a few tests to see what they really look like. Drag them out into the sunlight and then take a look. See if they actually have a reflection in the mirror you hold up to them.

Real relationships have definitive qualities. Sharing feelings builds intimacy. Being there in time of crisis builds faith. Being honest about what is or isn't working in your relationship creates the ties that bind and support. Relationships with energy vampires don't pass many of those thresholds. Instead, there is a lot of drama. Who doesn't love a good story about a bad boy? Why don't you pick up a book by Stephanie Meyer or Anne Rice, and read about vampires instead of having a relationship with one?

Men are especially good at getting your attention with this bad-boy energy. The difference between a sorcerer and a wizard is the sorcerer wants to get his energy from you and the wizard already gets it directly from God. Whom are you choosing to spend time with? I've known many married women who've been tempted by an outsider. I call it flash and trash. If you're married or the

man is married, the flash is something different and exciting. But then comes the trash. He can't leave his wife,
you can't leave your family (for X reasons), and no one's
building true intimacy with anyone because there is no
emotional honesty and very little real self-care. Hey, it
can be worth taking the journey with a sorcerer. There's
a lot to learn from darkness. All I'm saying is take down
the veils and take a good look at who and what you're
dealing with. It may take months or years to see the
truth, but the truth is always worth knowing.

Sorcerers come in all shapes and sizes. One more
notable characteristic is the desire to control and manage
people and circumstances around them. It gives them a
false sense of power. They play God without the godly
aspect of allowing free choice. Hmm . . . remind you of
anyone? A recent administration? Your spouse? Your
priest or minister? Sorcerer energy can manifest in exag-
gerated ways and in subtle ways. It's up to you to say no
to sorcerer energy from others and even some that comes
from within you. It's not up to you to change and fix it,
except in yourself. People who are well-versed sorcerers
don't have much capacity or desire to change. The rare
exceptions are those who've been substance addicted, got
sober, and worked a program. They transform from sorcerers to wizards. They go from outsourcing their energy
to hooking up directly to divine.

For the most part, I've had to walk away from sorcerers for my own sanity, safety, and happiness. The more
one says no to controlling aspects of people's personalities
and yes to divine, the more light and dark can integrate.
There are so many ways to manipulate and be manipulated. This stuff is tricky.

Next we'll get down to brass tacks and do an inventory of who is around us.

The first order of business is to take a look at your inner circle. Christ had his disciples. He had an entourage to buffer him from the rest of the world. He surrounded himself with people he liked, respected, and trusted. Sure, Judas ended up being a bit of a problem, but for the most part it was a good group. Who's in your inner circle? Are they a buffer or a pain in the neck? Do they energize you or leave you feeling drained? I'm not saying you won't have conflicts or things to work through with these people, but it needs to be an equal energy exchange.

Here are some questions to ask yourself about the people in your inner circle.

Do they have a sense of humor? We're not talking angry sarcasm here, but real humor.

Do they take responsibility for their behavior?

Do they have an intention for honest communication?

Do they want to have an equal energy exchange or are they attempting a power-over model? For example, do you often feel belittled after interacting with them?

For many years of my life, when I encountered a person practicing a power-over model, I would feel icky in my stomach. I had no mental framework for what was going on. Now, after therapy and working with my angels, I can identify it immediately. When it happens, I either choose to address it directly with the person (so that they don't get away with bad behavior without taking responsibility) or I just notice it and move away from them and the situation. It's not my job to fix someone else, but it is my job to stand up for myself and protect myself.

People who are extremely controlling often see others as an extension of themselves. I've found that trying to be seen or understood by these individuals is completely pointless. It's much more beneficial to move out of their arena and move toward people who are interested in real communication. We have all been on both sides of the equation. When we're feeling insecure or afraid, we can move into trying to control people and situations. That is where we rely on our egos and the way we think things should be, instead of allowing people to make their own choices and trusting divine to intervene. Here are some more questions you can ask yourself.

Am I trying to get my energy from others by trying to control and manage their behavior while avoiding my own feelings? (Sorcerer model)

Am I going directly to God for help? (Wizard's way)

Are others trying to control and manage me? (Sorcerer model)

Take the Middle Road and Stay in the Moment

Sometimes relationships call for extreme action, such as removing people from your inner circle or bringing in new ones. Another form of action involves staying flexible and awake while navigating the waves of your feelings, your perceptions, and the ever-changing dynamics of your relationships. Life and relationships are a moment-by-moment proposition. Being true to your feelings, perceptions, and the moment helps you stay awake for the journey and invigorates your life.

I've watched as friends, family members, and clients have gone through life-altering changes such as marriage, divorce, childbirth, children leaving for college, and career changes. But some of the biggest changes may be the subtler ones happening under your nose. Your partner may be changing, your children may be growing up, or you may have grown in maturity. One exercise I use in my classes is the duct tape conversation. It's a wonderful way to find out just how current you are with your loved ones. Set aside time for coffee or a soda to share with your partner, friend, or child. Ask them lots of questions. As they answer, imagine your mouth has duct tape on it. The only time the duct tape comes off is to ask them for more details about their answers. This is a great time to become the observer. You can notice your feelings as they talk and any thoughts and judgments you may have about what they're saying. You may also notice something new about them, something you've never noticed or heard before. The art of listening involves becoming an empty canvas and letting someone paint their version of a masterpiece with their words.

Making assumptions about someone or a situation is a form of going to sleep. It is living in the past and is also a kind of death energy. It reminds me of the scene in the movie *The Lion King* when the wise old baboon, Rafiki, thumps the lion, Simba, on the head with his stick.

Simba asks, "What was that for?"

Rafiki answers, "It doesn't matter, it's in your past." Then he laughs.

You're living in the now—wow! Let's call the present-moment drug "nowie wowie." This high doesn't dull your perception, however; it refines it. Staying in the moment enlivens your senses and helps you see. It is a form of psychic ability because you're not looking through the veils of assumption and judgment. You're truly seeing. It is also a beautiful opportunity to be awake for divine guidance, heavenly signs, and other forms of energetic communication.

Last week I was struggling with really *seeing* some people in my life. I seemed to be stuck in a lot of assumptions I had made about them. I was walking through a parking lot and happened to glance at someone's license plate holder. It said, "Life's fragile, handle it prayerfully." Within twenty-four hours, a psychic friend of mine was reminding me to ask my guides for more help in having clear sight. We get to ask for help with this stuff. Our angels are vision specialists.

I knew someone who thought her marriage was going smoothly. Somewhat out of the blue, she asked her guides to weigh in. Within days, she found signs that her husband's attention was wandering. She'd realized she'd been blind to some of the earlier signals that something wasn't right. When you ask to see, the angels answer. That cuts both ways. Having a new, fresh perspective also involves seeing the love and growth within a partner, lover, child, coworker, or friend. The point is that having the willingness to see is really a prayer to the universe to clear up our misperceptions. This prayer takes faith and courage. When we're willing to see the power and love within our spouse, we're willing to risk that that person may outgrow us or pull us forward on life's path. When we're wiling to see apparent flaws in our spouse, we're opening up to the idea we may need to make our own changes to help them grow. Seeing isn't for sissies. It's for those of you who want to get real and live life on the cutting edge. The good news is, a lot of what's up for seeing is about love—the love within others and the love between humans and their guides.

The universe is always moving us toward expansion. Having choices and broad ideas about what's possible keeps us in the flow. Divine is a big place with lots of room for change, growth, and movement in all directions. When we go into lockdown in our thinking about people and situations, there's no breathing room. There's no lightness. Offering more room in your perceptions allows in more light. It illuminates what's actually there, not just what you may believe is there. Imagine you have a love lamp. It's a torch burning with the flame of truth and light. Invite that torch into your life. Name some areas in your life you'd like to have illuminated. What gives? What's being revealed during your days? The information often comes through feedback from people, psychic images, or subtle signs (such as songs or bumper stickers). If you ask for illumination, your angels will answer. They're often quite ingenious and humorous in their methodology.

This chapter is about noticing, not necessarily running out and doing something about your energy patterns and relationships. It's about allowing the veils of illusion to lift. Once you really see the truth, the truth will set you free. God will guide you through these experiences and to your next best action steps. This is the journey of self-care.

Addiction and Hitchhikers

Addictions that affect you from the neck up (alcohol, pot, cocaine, and prescription drugs) can impair your brain and your psychic vision. Nothing is more desirable to an undesirable entity than someone with bad judgment who can't see. These dark entities float around drunks all the time. They are akin to demons and they love to attach themselves to addicts. Healers use the friendlier term "hitchhikers." These entities hitch a ride with someone who's asleep at the wheel, then guide the person to do their bidding. Hey, maybe that's why the movie *Hitcher,* starring Rutger Hauer, completely freaks me out. Picking up a hitchhiker is a form of being possessed and it isn't pretty.

There are obvious addictions and subtler ones. I stopped drinking nineteen years ago, but then came the onset of other bad habits. I turned to sex, drama, working, cigars, food, and over-mothering for a distraction. I still struggle with many of these issues. I've firmly decided not to give up cigars. They're a habit that took hold while I was an investigative reporter working in television news. Cigars are sensuous, outrageous, and delicious. I'm not giving them up, so there. That said, I have had to drop some other addictions because they often bring unwanted company.

With the intense and immense energies affecting the planet today, it's a good time to get clean and sober. If you can't do it on your own, then get help. Go to rehab, Alcoholics Anonymous, or a recovery counselor. You deserve clarity. Go ahead and bring your entities to the meetings as well; they'll hate it. Life's too short to be foggy and loaded down with hitchhikers. Once that's handled it is time to take a look at other subtler forms of addictions. All of them are distractions from quieting down and feeling our feelings. Here are a few favorite isms: materialism, workaholism, perfectionism, volunteerism, and eating too much (sorry can't think of the ism word for that). Experiencing your feelings is hard. It can be very uncomfortable. But it is also enlivening. My four-year-old expresses a hundred different versions of his feelings every day. And he's got an endless well of energy. He is in the flow; nothing is stuck.

Using feeling words when you talk to others or journal is an honest approach to communication. It keeps the focus on you and leads to real breakthroughs in your life. These days I can burst into tears when someone says something to me that hits a painful place in me. Years ago I would get mad and retaliate verbally or shrink into the corner. But that wasn't an honest root response. I was trying to cover up humiliation. I felt hurt. Today the hurt just bubbles to the surface, but it also helps raise the level of communication I have with my family.

Of course, addiction doesn't just impair us; it also impairs our loved ones. Keep your eyes open for odd behavior, hitchhikers, and a lack of presence coming from loved ones who may be in the throes of addiction. When you stay awake to the symptoms, it allows you to take appropriate actions to care for and protect yourself.

Seeing is believing. When you can see this stuff for yourself, you begin to believe in energy realms and that you truly are not alone. When you see the ghost and feel the ghost, you have new awareness that allows you to give the ghost the boot! You also see that sometimes people's words or physical images do not match up with their overall energy. Wake up, sleepyhead! It's time to fully participate in the life going on around you. The only way to stay safe and stay away from energy vampires is to accept their existence. The way to deal appropriately with your lover, spouse, child, or boss is to really see them first!

As Joe Friday said in the 1950s television series *Dragnet,* "Just the facts, ma'am." To get the facts, you have to open your eyes to see them. You have to open your ears to hear them. It's a physical, mental, and spiritual process. Allow yourself to have the courage and opportunity to see the truth of the situation. Allow yourself to feel your feelings while seeing the truth. Psychic housewives are rarely bored. There's too much flying around in their realm to keep track of once they open up psychically. If you're ready to expand your adventure, then do the following exercises. Ooh, this will be interesting!

Psychic Laundry List

This chapter's exercises are about waking up to what and who is around you, and acting accordingly. Take your time; these are all perception humdingers.

1. In meditation: Ask for complete protection. Ask for two days reprieve, where you only get information from your guides of highest consciousness that is information for and about you and no one else. See what you get and observe anything or anyone that seems to violate that request.

2. Post a psychic perimeter around your body, your home, and your work space. You can visualize a fence or post guard dogs, angels, or other guards—anything that comes to you to assist or protect. You can even set up alarms that go off psychically if someone is trying to get in. Then see who or what is trying to breach that protection.

3. What's your ghost situation? Are there any in the house? Do your kids talk about seeing or hearing them? Are you seeing or hearing them? If the answer is yes, try doing your own ghostbusting. Follow a few of the guidelines in this chapter and your own intuition to get rid of those unwanted houseguests.

4. Do a soul interview with a person you love. Get quiet, close your eyes, and imagine meeting up with that person in a comfortable setting. Ask them a question about something you've been wondering about. See what images appear. What do they tell you visually or with their words in your meditation?

5. Next, conduct an in-person interview with the same person. Imagine you have duct tape on your mouth. Listen to what they're saying. Ask them more questions; get more details about what they're telling you. Don't overtly react emotionally to what they're saying, even if it shocks you. Save your reaction for later, with a friend. Nod, say, "Tell me more," but don't interrupt them. This is your chance to really see who's there in

front of you. It is also an opportunity to see if your psychic interview matches up with your in-person experience.

6. Finally, list your possible addictions. Are any of them affecting you from the neck up? How about your loved ones? Are you sensing their addictions as well? This is the chapter to get real about it. Start seeing what's influencing your ability to really see. I strongly recommend getting sober when it comes to drugs and alcohol. That prevents the hitchhikers from hitching up to your wagon.

✦Chapter 5✦
Wacky Tools to Enhance the Ride

No, this is not the part of the book where I talk about witches' brooms or marital sex toys. That comes later. . . . I'm kidding, OK?

If you're going into the deep end of the pool, why not do it as smoothly as possible, perhaps using some floaties and a kickboard? You might want to consider new tools to enhance your life and your energy work. Reiki energy, pendulums, crystals, icons, altars, and bathing with sea salt can all enhance the divine road trip.

Reiki, Pendulums, and Crystals

How about getting certified in Reiki? This is an energetic healing practice that comes from Japan. When you are initiated into it, you become familiar with an energy that can heal you and others. Some people believe Reiki raises your vibration and makes psychic information more accessible. Some of my friends have become certified in Reiki and they love the way the training has impacted their lives. They've tapped the energy to heal pets and children, help art projects flow, and improve their own mental clarity. If the word "Reiki" resonates with you and the concept appeals, I highly recommend taking a course in it.

Another tool of the psychic trade is the pendulum. Most metaphysical stores and even some mainstream bookstores are carrying pendulums now. Metal ones are the simplest because sometimes crystal ones absorb other energies and lose their objectivity after extended use. Here's how it works: You hold the pendulum in your dominant hand and ask a question. Call in your guides of highest consciousness first, to make sure you're calling in beings of light. The pendulum will usually wind up by going back and forth in a straight line, and then it will begin a circular turn. If the turn is clockwise, the answer is yes (according to the method I was taught). If the turn is counterclockwise, the answer is no. If it just goes back and forth, there is no answer yet because the timing is wrong to even ask the question. The method takes practice. The idea is to keep your hand as still as possible and to let the energy move the pendulum. If it is a question on a topic that is emotionally charged for you, it may not work. When I'm upset, I sometimes get answers that turn out to be inaccurate. When I'm somewhat calm, I like to sit around and ask ridiculous questions just to see what I get.

Guides of highest consciousness . . .

Was I a complete ass the other day while talking to Jon?

Yes.

Are my thighs the biggest they've ever been?

Yes.

Will that ever change?

Yes.

Is it OK if I have some more coffee?

Big NO!

You get the picture.

I also use the pendulum in gift buying. I'll hold it over the gift I'm considering for a person and see what it says. I had waited until the last minute to buy my dad a present for his seventy-fifth birthday. A few days before the big day, I heard angels singing in an aisle in Wal-Mart. There was a folding chair with my dad's college logo on it. I got out my pendulum and got a big clockwise circle (yes). My dad loves that chair. He put it in his garage office and sits in it to go through his file cabinets. I'm telling you, the pendulum takes the worry out of last-minute shopping.

Now let's move on to the topic of crystals. There are many books out there on the subject. One of the most thorough is the Melody book *Love Is in the Earth.* Other good ones include books by Katrina Raphael and the book *Moldavite,* by Robert Simmons and Kathy Warner. You don't have to have crystals to take this trip. But they do help pave the way for a powerful journey. I have gone on many a crystal quest. My guides have sent me out to get a certain crystal at a certain time at an exact place for a specific person. They've done it repeatedly. I've spent as little as a dollar and as much as thirteen hundred dollars for a crystal. I bought the expensive crystal for my friend Helen Michaels as a gift and put it on my credit card. I was called by spirit to do so. My body just pulled me to the store and I bought it on the spot after consulting my pendulum. That crystal went on to play a highly significant role energetically in the lives of Helen, her family, friends, and many of her clients. It has transformative qualities that just keep on giving.

Another time, I arrived at an amazing crystal shop that was closed. They'd just received a shipment from Brazil and were sorting through it. The owner let me in and, using my pendulum, I searched the room and found one crystal in an unopened barrel. The other I found by telling the owner I'd had a dream about a blue crystal. He came out of his office, holding a clear quartz crystal; he told me it was called a blue ray crystal. He really made me work for it, though, I tell you. I had been in his shop for more than an hour before he finally brought it out. He is a gatekeeper and doesn't let just anyone buy certain stones. While holding that blue ray crystal, I was able to access many different realms that were difficult to hear before. It seemed to act as an antenna, taking the signals and putting them into terms or language I could understand. If there is a crystal calling your name, you will be pulled to it or it will land in your lap. They each have their own unique life force, personality, and power. They also have a magnetic draw that will lead you right to them.

Many are drawn to stones as they begin their psychic journey. Let's go over the properties of the following starter crystals. Here are the types of crystals that might be calling to you and why:

AMETHYST is purple in color and has transformative powers.

ROSE QUARTZ is pink and is a heart opener.

HEMATITE is a silvery stone that grounds you.

BLACK TOURMALINE is a stone that offers grounding and deflects negativity.

CITRINE is a yellow stone that attracts wealth and deflects negativity.

MOLDAVITE is a green crystal from a meteorite that helps you to accept your role as a cosmic visitor who's chosen to make Earth home. It can also speed up your soul's journey of learning and finding purpose here on Earth. It's a powerful crystal that can really kick your behind. If it's too much, you'll lose it. I know half a dozen people who have lost their moldavite pieces. The stone knows when it is overpowering you, so it splits the scene.

SELENITE is a milk-colored stone that brings a tremendous amount of light into your body and life.

OBSIDIAN is black, grounding, and can put you in touch with darker energies that complement the lighter ones.

CLEAR QUARTZ has too many qualities to list. I find its most prominent role to be fine-tuning messages from your guides.

I highly recommend these crystals as starter stones on your journey. They grow with you. You do not need to go out and get any of them, however. This list is just to help you with an awareness of them. Any crystals that want to be with you will find their way into your heart and home. It will just happen. These are the ultimate pet rocks—although they are a bit more like wild animals! They have their own freewheeling energy and they command reverence and respect. Crystals can enhance the psychic journey. They help transform negativity, heal addictions, ground you, and bring light into your life. These stones can set the tone that allows you to take the next baby step on your spiritual path.

Icons, Altars, and Rituals

One big benefit to having your higher self behind the

wheel is feeling relief that you don't have to do every-thing yourself. You keep your feet on the ground, your head in the stars, and leave the driving to divine. A lot of the journey is letting go, letting God, and building a practice that centers on effortlessness. Icons, altars, and rituals can facilitate the movement of energy without you doing a whole lot. There are hundreds of ways to set up all three. Following your intuition is the best approach.

Good ol' Mother Mary or a statue of Kuan Yin can help save the day. When you wake up feeling concerned about getting through the next few hours with your kids, take emergency measures. Grab tea light candles, light them, and put them in front of an icon. Let them do the heavy lifting. Wait a minute, wait a minute, am I sug-gesting idol worship? Nope. I'm suggesting this technique as a way to call in the energy that these icons represent. Mary offers the energy of allowing and Kuan Yin provides the energy of compassion. Other examples of energy icons could be a plastic German shepherd for protection or a fairy to represent inviting more fairy magic into your life. Lighting candles in front of them lights a flame of consciousness around these energies. That allows divine to do the heavy lifting and allows you to get on with your day.

Perhaps you've already brought statuary into your home. If not, run an experiment. Head to your local church or new age store or Web retailer and see what you're drawn to. Perhaps statuary of Jesus, Mary, Archangel Raphael, Saint Michael, or Saint Joe will catch your fancy. Buy one, place it on your mantel at home, light some candles around it when times get tough, and see what happens. The proof of the pudding is in the eating. If this practice doesn't bring relief as I suggest, chuck the statue and this book with it. It may, however, prove the truth of the oxymoronic phrase I've come to cherish: "effortless results." When you release your woes to a being of love and compassion, wonderful results can and do occur.

Most of my work with rituals came through my intuition, but many books about Wiccan traditions have similar ideas spelled out in their pages. Working in and with nature is extremely powerful and magical. Here's an example: I set an intention about where I wanted my family to live. I wrote it with permanent marker on a seashell. I planned to throw it into the ocean. As I parked at the beach, I realized that I needed to be more open to other plans for my family. I felt called to smash the seashell in a cloth and dump the pieces into the sea. I said a prayer asking for highest good and tossed the shell bits into the surf. I then lay down on the beach, said some prayers, and meditated. I then walked back to where I'd thrown the shell and there at my feet was a new white shell that had just washed ashore. It was as if the sea had transmuted the energy and form (the certain form I wanted) and sent back a clean slate. It gave me chills.

Nature does for us what we cannot do for ourselves. If you are feeling intruded upon by people or circumstances, head outdoors and grab a stick. Draw a circle around yourself and say:

Circle of Light
Burning Bright
Let it Be
Blessed Be

Imagine a protective circle of fire surrounding you. Another way to work with nature and allow nature to work with you is to lie on the ground. Imagine releasing your fears into the earth for transmutation and ask to receive the healing energy of the earth in exchange. Mother Earth appreciates it because you end up carrying her energy into the world.

Another prayer I highly recommend is one my grandmother taught me when I was a girl. It is the Unity Church Prayer of Protection:

> This Light of God Surrounds Me
> The Love of God Enfolds Me
> The Power of God Protects Me
> The Presence of God Watches over Me
> Wherever I Am, God Is!

It is a handy prayer to say for yourself and your children. When my mother was in her twenties, she was working as a flight attendant. One of her flights went through a powerful storm while the plane was crossing the Pacific Ocean. They had terrible turbulence. At that very hour, my grandmother woke from a sound sleep and began saying the Unity Prayer of Protection for my mother. The plane made the trip safely and my mother was fine. The power of prayer and the psychic mother–daughter connection are both evident to me from that story. I keep a copy of that prayer on our mantel in the living room.

Following your own gut to create your own rituals is part of the plan for psychic development. Go out into nature or even your backyard and find out what's calling to you. Throwing rocks or sticks that symbolize your troubles into a stream or river can represent washing your troubles away. Jumping into the ocean can be a way to cleanse your body and your soul. Saying prayers together with people over the phone or while holding their hand is a way to power up your request to God.

Praying at dinnertime creates an attitude of gratitude. If I forget to pray, our four-year-old inevitably pipes up and asks for a dinner prayer. Give thanks for your abundance and have everyone in the family take a turn leading the prayer. A dinner blessing protects and enhances mealtime energy. It contributes to a supper that is full of grace.

Grab a crystal tuning bowl, a drum, chimes, or a flute and make some music. Music and rhythmic sound allow your soul to sing and the angels to call right back to you. My kids love to help make music in the house with those simple instruments. The whole house feels lighter as the sound moves through our home. One time, my friend Peggy who is Native American grabbed a drum in our house and started pounding on it. She was drumming the Grandmother's song. It's a chant she drums to at women's ceremonies. The song changed the feeling throughout our house for several days. It was as if an elder were among us, comforting us with her wisdom. Drumming, dancing, and chanting are ways to invite music into our bodies and souls to clear and enliven us. Playing a compact disc that features chanting is also a way to clear negative energies in your house. Your home is a sacred place. It's where you and your family play together, pray together, laugh, cry, and yell. Lots of big feelings can happen at home. That's why energetically clearing out the place on a regular basis can help with the flow.

Freshwater and Sea Salt Baths

I love to bathe in spring water. At our place up north, we have a horse trough outside the house and a hose that we hook up to the laundry sink. Woods surround our house, giving us lots of privacy. I bathe outside in the fresh water and sunlight. Our four-year-old also loves to sit outside and play in the bath. My older kids are a bit shy about using it, so they head for a swim in the river. We are blessed to have fresh spring water running to our house. Nothing beats a spring water bath outside in the sun in both summer and winter.

Chances are good that you might not have the same opportunity because the neighbors would report you, so how about soaking in a sea salt bath in the tub? If soaking in salt feels too drying, use essential oils instead. Explore their properties and see what fits for you at the time. Keeping at least four different oils on hand is an important form of physical and spiritual self-care. Soaking in your bathroom tub with salt or essential oils is a fundamental technique for clearing and renewing your body's energy. It's also a solution for those living in the city. A horse trough probably wouldn't fit on the front porch of your house and it might make the neighbors really nervous.

Energy Work and Massage

Healing energy work can make your psychic journey a lot simpler. It is incredibly helpful when you are making vibrational transitions. When more light energy is coming into your body, it's nice if someone can help smooth the transition. It's best to find someone by personal referral. That's how most people find doctors and therapists. It's important to treat finding an energy worker with as much discernment. Massage and Reiki can get the stuck energy that is trapped in your muscles moving again. It is a great way to feel pampered and every mommy deserves that. It's also a message to the universe that says, "I deserve all this good," so that more can come to you.

The idea in this chapter is to let physical items, heavenly helpers, prayers, and boundaries do some of your energy work for you. Conserving energy is the name of the game on this path. Icons can act like homing beacons to the energy you're requesting. You are setting up a tangible symbol to pull in support for your day or situation. The visual cue also allows your brain to connect with and then release your concerns to something outside yourself. Doing rituals such as drawing a circle of protection, saying a prayer of protection, or saying a dinner prayer focused on gratitude also helps move energy around. Done on a regular basis, these actions can invigorate your day and create miracles. You are setting your intention in a physical way, which resonates throughout the earth's energies and comes back to you in physical form.

Making your home a safe space by regularly clearing the house with sage and music also sends the universe a message. You are saying that your home operates at a certain high vibration. You are affirming it as a safe place to have feelings, a place where family members connect with divine, and a home filled with fun and laughter. Preserving your home space is a way of energetically protecting yourself and your family members.

Bringing in physical tools such as icons is a simple way of enhancing your spiritual journey. Reiki training, pendulums, and crystals also set the tone for you and your home environment. Wearing crystals out in the world is a way to take a certain vibration with you to set a higher vibration for your interactions. Taking clearing, relaxing herbal or salt baths is a way to assist your body on this journey. These tools marry the physical and spiritual realms. For many reasons, we moms tend to hold off on this kind of self-care. Everyone benefits when mom gets all the support she can. Take this dare and do self-care.

Psychic Laundry List

This lesson is about letting the universe do for you! You deserve it. Physical tools can really assist you in growing spiritually and opening up psychically. Try at least half of the following suggestions. See what results you get by letting go and letting the universal energies take on some of your concerns. This is like hiring a nanny to take care of your problems.

1. Get a cardboard toilet paper roll and paint or color a design on the outside. Mine has black and white paint, representing yin and yang or positive and negative force in the universe. Put some sea salt in the roll and seal the ends with plastic wrap and a rubber band. This is your transformer. Whenever something is really bugging you, mentally send it through the roll. I've had some real miracles come from doing this.

2. Go to a crystal/stone store and let a crystal choose you. It will if you're ready. When you bring your crystal home, it is important to clear its energy. Place the crystal in a bowl outside, cover it with spring water, throw in some sea salt, and let it sit in the sunshine for at least ten minutes. Set it somewhere special in your house. Light a candle and put it in front of the stone and say a prayer of surrender.

3. Get or make a God or Goddess box. That's where you write what's on your mind or what you're attached to on paper and put it in the box. Then you release it.

4. Write someone's name or the name of a situation that you are feeling upset about. Then burn it. That releases your connection to it.

5. Buy some old plates at a garage sale or secondhand store. Write down topics on them with permanent marker and smash them with a hammer. This is my favorite—a big energy release!!

6. Find a stick, go outside, and draw a circle around you with the stick. As you do this, repeat the circle prayer: Circle of Light / Burning Bright / Let it Be / Blessed Be.

7. Head to a new age or church bookstore and see what icons are calling your name. Does Mary appeal? How about Buddha or Jesus? Perhaps a fairy? Or maybe you have something at home, such as a child's toy, a ceramic dog or snake, or something cute and cuddly. All can represent the energy you want to bring into your life. Light tea candles in front of the items and see what unfolds in your life.

8. Take a bath and soak up some essential oils or take a sea salt bath to clear your energies. Sometimes when you're at your kids' school, work, or the store, you pick up unwanted energies. The bath can wash your troubles away.

9. Sign up to become Reiki certified.

10. Practice with a pendulum. See where it takes you and if you get accurate and helpful information. Round and round it goes, where it lands, nobody knows.

These techniques may seem goofy but they really work. They allow your ego to let go and the universe and your higher self to step in to help.

✦✦Chapter 6✦✦
You Know, for Kids

This is the chapter where we hire you a divine nanny for your kids. Whoops, it's already been done! Your kids have a squadron of mature heavenly helpers and baby angels. They also have, just as you do, an all-knowing higher self/soul guiding their journey. Actually, in this chapter, we're going to open the doors to an old-fashioned one-room schoolhouse. It's painted red and inside has desks and a blackboard. Imagine you're the teacher in the old West and your kids are just in from recess and exploring their environment. You decide the best way to instruct them is to find out what they already know. You have them draw what they've seen, talk about what they experienced outside, and go through a picture book to prompt their thoughts and memories. This is exactly the method you use to discover what your kids already know about the unseen and help them cope with that information. This is about being a facilitator. By giving your kids language and freedom to talk about their experiences, you create a schoolroom that is a safe place for exploration.

So your youngest is seeing ghosts and is now officially freaked out. So is Mom. That's to be expected. Ghosts can be spooky! There's good news, though: Often the most obvious sign of psychic ability is someone seeing a ghost. Along with seeing ghosts come many other forms of psychic abilities that can really support your kids. As they open up psychically, kids can sense danger, they can be intuitively drawn to wonderful people and experiences, and they can hear their angels. Now that spirit has your attention, it's time to equip yourself with information and tools. That's how you successfully mother a psychic child.

Some of the best information about energy and psychic ability comes directly from the kid's own guides and from Mom. Take out an angel deck and play it with your kids. At my house, each of my kids takes a turn pulling three cards from a full deck. I'm always surprised by what comes of the experience. The ideas on each card, such as divine guidance, personal power, or laughter, reveal interesting parts of my children. They will talk about experiences at school that relate to the cards and how they see divine energy in their lives. They don't use big words to explain it, but the meaning is there. When we're done with that, we like to play a game of sudden death. We collapse the deck and deal. Each of us pulls an angel card from the deck. The first person to pull three naked angels is out of the game. Don't worry, the cards are tastefully decorated with baby angels and angels with scarves around their private areas. The kids thought of the game and always get a big giggle out of playing it.

My kids also love the animal divination decks. My son continuously pulls the deer card and the dragonfly, which have messages about standing quietly in your divine power and believing in yourself. My daughter often pulls the wolf card (strength and courage) and my youngest gets the coyote card (spiritual trickster). The cards are beautiful reflections of their spirits. And I believe the angel card messages encourage the kids to see their true natures. They provide insights to me about some of my kids' struggles and victories in their spiritual realms and everyday lives. We end up having amazing and silly times with the divination cards. They are always thrilled to play with the decks.

An important reason why I wrote this book is to support you in supporting your kids to be fully psychic. So many mommies in my classes and reading sessions have kids who see ghosts or spirit guides. When my daughter was five and I was just opening up psychically, she told me there were two strangers at the end of her bed. When I looked, I saw the ghosts as well. I cleared her room and our house and told them not to come back. As I've mentioned, there are many talents besides the ability to see ghosts to be experienced in the psychic realm.

My son Nathan specializes in manifesting. After we saw the movie *Transformers,* he started pretending he was a motorcycle that transformed into a robot. There is no such character in the movie. At a store, we discovered a motorcycle transformer toy. It was the only one on the shelf and I bought it for him. On the escalator, he said, "I'm good at manifesting, Mom."

It has happened over and over with him. He says he wants a play date and two different friends will call to arrange one within days. He wanted a new sweatshirt and his grandparents sent one in the mail the same week. His list goes on and on.

My daughter Kendall gets psychic images that show

up in cartoon form. One time I asked if we should stop in a certain town on a road trip. She closed her eyes and immediately saw a big-eyed baboon with a quizzical look, which I took to mean, "I have no idea," but it was very funny imagery from her guides.

Another time I asked if she got anything psychic about my job search, which wasn't progressing well. Before I had finished the question, she told me she saw bamboo and a rhino. I asked her to explain. She said she read recently that bamboo takes about five years to mature, but once it does, its roots are deep and tower over the other plants. I knew immediately that the guides were referencing the fact that I'd been psychic (at the time) for five years. They were telling me that I was just moving into a period of maturity with my abilities and that patience was in order. She also told me that the rhino is an endangered species. I could relate. At that moment, I was feeling endangered. I was a psychic mom trying to make a living as a healer and reenter the work force with an unorthodox background. I was short on funds and felt alone with my gift. The guides were correct—I was feeling endangered. I think Kendall was ten when she told me all of this. She has a gift and a very powerful sense of herself in the world.

Our four-year-old son, Sam, is all about superheroes. He loves to play Superman and Spider-Man. I've learned a lot about the hero's journey by watching the movies and shows he loves to watch and by watching him play. Sam just knows things and was definitely a psychic baby. Before he was born, a baby came to me, lying on his back with his hands behind his head. To this day Sam sleeps like that. The baby told me that his right ear would be bigger than his left ear, but I shouldn't worry about it. Sam's right ear is bigger than his left ear. In one of the pictures on my website, I have a picture of Sam playing guns at Whitney Portal in California. In the picture, there appears to be a blue spaceship above Sam. When Sam sees the picture he says, "Look, there's the spaceship."

One time my husband, Sam, and I were headed to a psychic fair at a place in Southern California called Harmony Grove. Sam was very animated, talking a mile a minute. I said, "Sam, are you excited because you're going to see a bunch of psychics?"

"Ha," Sam said, "amateurs!"

I turned to my husband in the car in complete shock and asked him, "Did he just say amateurs?"

"Yes," my husband said, "he sure did."

Even for me, a professed psychic mom, that was pretty freaky.

What's clear to me is that when I allow my kids the freedom to see and engage with the spiritual dimension, they lead me on the path as well. All of my kids believe in magical creatures, ghosts, spirit guides, and the ability to manifest what they want. They also believe in a very loving universal force. I feel very privileged that these amazing souls have come into my life. The more I hear about today's children and their psychic and intuitive abilities, the more it becomes apparent we're living in a special time.

They're Divinely Hooked Up

Today's children are entering their bodies with their spiritual connection intact. The challenge for today's parents is to allow this to be. This kind of knowing comes and goes directly from the heart and not the head. It is powerful and it takes a healthy, healing adult parent to allow its magnificence.

Do these kids still need boundaries? Absolutely. They still need loving discipline. But an innate ability to self-correct is also inherent in their spirituality. They have such a direct connection to divine. When I do readings and see some of these kids' angels and guides, I'm blown away. The amount of wisdom, love, and generosity in their heavenly teams is unparalleled. It's like having a combo fairy godmother/nanny that guides them through good times and bad. These are immense angels who wrap their wings around our kids with such love and com-passion that it brings tears to my eyes. Many young chil-dren know that they have heavenly helpers, and they can often describe their guides in detail. Knowing that these children have personal angels should offer some relief to all of us moms. We really don't have to do it all; the kids are watched over by angels. We are only our children's stewards. When we truly let go and let God, our kids flourish. They came to Earth with a heavenly support team already in place. The more we as parents support that divine connection, the more we can relax on this crazy journey of life.

Kids see things that we don't. Children see fairies. Children swim in their imagination, which is where mag-ical creatures live and breathe. Two young friends of mine who are seven and nine explained to me about their experience with fairies. They were constantly find-ing tiny glittering plastic balls around on the ground in their neighborhood. They told me the fairies had left the balls for the girls to find. They also explained that there are good fairies and bad ones. And they told me a bad fairy had cast a spell on one of their friends. I asked them how you break a bad fairy spell. Miranda looked at me like I must be an idiot not to know and answered politely, "With pomegranate juice, of course."

I've come to believe that pomegranates do break bad fairy spells. My guides have told me it's a great way to bring in positive energy to your body. Interestingly, pomegranate as a flavor in all sorts of commercial drinks and foods has exploded in popularity in the past few years.

A mommy I know has a daughter who sees fairies. The girls in her class even call her a fairy girl. Kids have no hesitation about saying their truth. The only problem is their parents don't always see the unseen, so they don't call it the truth. If you have kids who see ghosts, fairies, and/or angels, tell your kids it's wonderful, because it truly is. But it's also important to remind them that not all children or adults believe in this stuff. To protect them from teasing, it's important that they only tell friends and adults they trust. The best place to talk about topics related to psychic ability is at home; it is to be hoped that your home is a safe environment for you and your family to explore your psychic experiences.

Sentient Kids

Some children have very sensitive natures when it comes to being in public or with lots of other children at school. These kids are sentient. That means they absorb other people's energy or pick up on the vibrations of a place that has nothing to do with them personally. Signs of this can include an upset stomach, crying for no apparent reason, or completely shutting down. These kids should not be overscheduled. They should be allowed time to relax and retreat. That may mean watching a video, reading a book, having a play date with just one other child, going into nature or to the local park for some play, or spending time alone in their room for a while after school or big social events.

Keep an eye out for signs your child is sensitive to the feelings of others, then act accordingly. Try suggesting that your sensitive kids put up a protective bubble around themselves. That tells the universe they need space and protection. Calling in extra energetic help is a good habit for kids with psychic abilities to develop. And since you're having psychic experiences, who better to teach them these tools than you? The best advocate they have for their souls are their guides and you, their psychic housewife mom.

Knowing your kids means knowing what they see in the unseen world. When you are curious without judgment, it allows them to open up and explore their psychic abilities. It's also an opportunity to see their talents, whether those talents are manifesting, seeing fairies, talking to ghosts, or feeling other people's feelings. Seeing ghosts can feel scary to kids, but having you around to protect them and help them understand that these abilities are relatively normal can ease the anxiety. Having you encourage them to manifest, do energy protection, and retreat when they need to can make the psychic journey a lot easier for your little ones. Helping them find tools, such as simple divination card decks, crystals, and fairy, angel, or dragon statues, also assists them on their energetic journey. Open up the lines of communication and get out the psychic tools. Psychic school is now in session.

Psychic Laundry List

In this week's exercises, psychic school is in session for your kids.

1. Talk to your kids about what they "see" and "hear" in the world of the unseen. Ask them about their dreams and what they think the dreams mean. If they mention seeing ghosts or deceased relatives, get curious. What are these people saying? What do they look like? Making this a regular part of your family's week sets a positive tone about psychic and intuitive experiences and opens the doors of communication. Purchase a simple angel deck or animal totem deck. Have your kids take turns spreading the cards and pulling between one and three cards. Read the meanings of the symbols they pulled and talk about them. How does that card apply to recent events or emotional experiences in their lives?

2. As adults, we know that not everyone believes in psychic abilities, intuition, and magical creatures. If your child is school age, tell them they're welcome to talk openly at home about this stuff, but they don't have to talk about it with their friends or teachers unless they feel comfortable doing so. Part of creating a safe environment for the kids is helping them understand that not everyone sees or believes in this stuff.

3. Take your kids to a store with crystals, magical creatures, statues, and drums or crystal bowls. See what they are drawn to in the store. Buy them one or two special items to have in their room, to remind them of the world of energy. They and their guides know what they need and want. Let them take the lead. It can be a very magical (and inexpensive) shopping trip.

4. Pay special attention to how your kids react to being around crowds or certain public places. If they seem to be shutting down, they may be overexposed to some negative energy. Work with your kids to put up energetic protection and give them limited time in environments that make them extremely uncomfortable.

✦Chapter 7✦
Going Down the Road with Your Psychic Abilities

So, now that we've piled the kids in the limo along with your angel team and human team, and you've put your higher self behind the wheel, how's it going? Road tripping with divine can be . . . well, a trip! You can feel nuts, like you really don't know who you are or where you're going. You may find you have a lot of back-seat drivers yelling at you and a few people watching the car swerve, slow down, and then speed up who have now concluded you might be crazy. This is the chapter where I hope to reassure you that looking crazy does not mean being crazy, that you really do have natural psychic abilities, and that it takes practice to recognize and get comfortable with your psychic gifts.

You've seen ghosts, you've had accurate glimpses into the future, and your library is filling up with books about psychic abilities and crystals. Your days are numbered. Eventually, your husband and mother-in-law will know the truth—that you've gone stark raving mad! You're already thinking it, so let's just say it out loud. You're sure it's only a matter of time before someone reports you to child protective services or your local priest.

"Surely, someone can help this woman and set her straight," you hear your inner judge and jury declare.

Honey, I have some bad news. Divine light, love, and truth won't be stifled or stay in the closet for long. As they say in Alcoholics Anonymous, you are only as sick as your secrets. The more you try to hide what's coming out in your life, the sloppier it gets. The energy is already wild, uncontrollably silly, and attention-seeking. Imagine you're back in your twenties and your totally reckless and completely embarrassing fifteen-year-old sister is talking to you and your date. You can't hide your sister in the closet; that kind of energy wants out. It's the same with spiritual energy. It wants out and is about to be seen by friends and strangers.

Many women avoid the odyssey of spiritual self-discovery because they want guarantees about outcome. They want the journey to be a neat, acceptable package with a lovely bow on top. The only thing you're guaranteed on this journey is a wild ride. And you can be assured that following divine guidance and allowing your psychic abilities to flourish can look and feel incredibly sloppy! Many of us fear that if we proceed, we'll lose our loved ones in the process. It's like taking your family to the Jurassic Park ride at Universal Studios. They'll either board the boat with you or stay behind and look at the pictures they take of you screaming, thrilled, and sopping wet. They do not have to come with you. But they usually do. Because they love you and trust the choices you make for yourself.

Silliness can be one of the best antidotes to fear. Go ahead and be willing to make fun of yourself and your journey. Grab a crystal ball and a head scarf; be a gypsy fortune teller for Halloween. Leave out a giant crystal the next time your mom drops by unannounced. This isn't as serious as you might believe. Talking about it out loud, living it, and laughing about it make psychic abilities easier to stomach. I'm not saying you have to blab your beliefs across your kids' school grounds. But standing up for what you believe and see is an important pursuit. It is a key to walking in your truth and integrity. And laughing about all of it helps to ease your fears.

Throughout history, women have been persecuted for following their feminine intuition, nature's cycles, and ebbing emotional tides. But those energies are now emerging all around us. You have an important role of divine discovery and self-discovery. Your courage to pursue your dreams is noticed in heaven. You are being asked to be completely honest. The beings of light are asking you to follow your heart and speak your truth. You may feel incredibly vulnerable, but there is divine protection in place. The most important boundary you can set is not permitting others to intentionally interrupt your journey. As the veils of illusion fall, you will see the truth about people and situations in your life. That is a form of protection. Some will react strongly to your newfound psychic abilities. Whether you have to put up a good fight with your critics or walk away peacefully, God's got your back. This is a place where complete trust is required. Say a prayer for peace, protection, humor, and the courage to be authentic. This isn't a journey for wimps. But as the sign on my dining room wall says: "You can't scare me, I have children."

Your Innate Abilities

Some psychics out there try to tell you that they have special abilities that no else has and make money doing readings, appearing on television shows, and writing books telling you how special they are. They really infuriate me. I'm tired of the message they and their handlers propagate, that is, that there's an exclusive club of psychics, and you can't get into it. Many of these people promote the idea that they've had the gift since childhood, and that they are unique. Their appointments are booked five years out and their readings cost as much as a monthly car payment. Your internal psychic is more available and there's no charge to access her. Of course, there are many professional psychics who give great information and offer authentic lessons to others about accessing their own guides. I'm just grousing about the ones who insinuate that being psychic is an exclusive club.

All of us have had the "gift" our entire lives. It's all about the degree to which you and your family environment either encouraged it to flourish or squashed it. It's also about divine timing. Safety first, and a child knows when it doesn't feel safe to see ghosts, angels, or bright aura colors. I invite you to close your eyes and relax and remember a few childhood memories in which spirit and intuitions were alive and well in your life.

I remember when I was about ten, I looked in the mirror at myself and heard the words "I love you." I knew it was from an energy that was a caretaker. Over time and after a lot of childhood trauma, I no longer believed in that voice or remembered its presence. Years later in my twenties, I did a guided meditation in a spiritual class during which I met a female guide in a garden. She handed me a beautiful box and when I opened it, inside was a heart with the words "I love you." Around my forty-first birthday, my friend Helen Michaels made me a beautiful box. The outside was decorated with angel figurines and paintings from nature. On the top was a baby held by angels. She told me I was that baby, cared for by great beings. When I opened the box, inside was a heart with the inscription *Je t'aime* ("I love you," in French).

At the time, my psychic abilities were already coming to fruition. But with that box came the memory of being loved and watched over by a spirit guide when I was a child. It brought many, many tears as I remembered that love and how I'd chosen to push it away. I remembered as a child being incredibly sensitive to other people's pain and sorrow. But in my household, the language of feelings was not always spoken. If I cried during an episode of *Lassie,* my grandparents (who helped raise me in the early years) told me to stop the tears or the show would be turned off. Feelings are the language of the soul and little people are linguistic experts. But as you are taught to control, manage, and suppress your feelings, the spark of intuition and self-trust is extinguished. Left to their own intuition, children do not hesitate to tell you when a place feels spooky and when they do or do not like a person's energy. They get strong feelings that a toy or an adventure is coming into their lives. These are all the seeds of psychic abilities.

As adults, we run instances such as the previous through our intellect and suppress our intuition before it catches its breath. Being willing to "be" is the first step in this journey and continues to be an essential aspect of the psychic pathway. We are revealing certain psychic abilities that have always been with us. We're learning to treat them as small vulnerable children. We pick them up, hug them, and tell them it is safe to come out to play. When we allow our psychic abilities to flourish and quit trying to deny them or cover them up, that's when the miracles happen. Taking a position that you are allowing spirit to be revealed is a powerful position. It's far more magical and efficient to not be heavily ego-involved, but to be heavenly evolved. Simply put, you become a master of letting go and letting God. You allow your true psychic self to emerge.

The Sixth Sense

Really seeing means using all of your senses. We've been sold a bill of goods that says what we perceive with our five senses is all that is there. But using your sixth sense is how you get the full picture. You can be deceived by people's words and even by their actions, but your gut feeling or your psychic sense of what's going on is the truth. It helps keep you from being manipulated by appearances.

Divine information comes in concisely. There are usually analogies or symbolic pictures to boil down the information. Sometimes you might require help in deciphering it. Sometimes it is completely obvious (like a stop sign or a green light). Whatever you get, get it down on paper. In the beginning of this journey, writing down the psychic information you receive can be extremely helpful. Often you will forget what's come in or it may not make sense at the time. Journaling about it allows you to remember it and see its context or meaning at a later date. Journaling also helps to make the information more tangible.

Your Psychic Style

We've talked about seeing external signs, getting images in your mind's eye, and hearing words as forms of psychic abilities. There are also body signals, such as your basic gut feeling about situations. Identifying your talents in these areas is important in accepting and nurturing your psychic abilities. Psychic information can come in a way that makes you feel very uncomfortable. If you sense events or the feelings of others, for instance, you will tend to feel like you're in the middle of a situation, even if the event is not happening to you personally. I'll give you some examples.

One time I was giving a reading to someone who had questions about some details of a fatal car accident he had been involved in. Suddenly, I was inside his pickup truck, holding a cigarette. It was night and I could see the other car coming at me. I could see the turn in the road and feel his apprehension. I was there at the scene in the driver's body. It was fascinating and uncomfortable at the same time. He confirmed all the details I was seeing, which was affirming for me. But I also felt his terror, right before he hit the other vehicle.

Another incident happened one night when my husband was working later than usual. I was in our Los Angeles house and I suddenly felt very afraid. I felt so scared, in fact, that I hid a large knife under our mattress before I went to bed. Then I had the thought of how awful it would be to have your throat slit. I wondered, why in the world am I thinking about this?

The next morning I happened to see a local television news story about a murder at a corporate parking structure in Los Angeles. A woman had been murdered on

her way to her car. Someone had slit her throat. My paranoid thoughts were another form of psychic knowing.
You actually feel the feelings of someone else. To me, it
can be a trying way to get information. It can be confusing to separate which feelings are about your own life
and which are feelings coming from someone else.

People who pick up on the feelings of others are often
resistant to allowing in their psychic abilities. They've got
enough big feelings of their own. Why experience the
feelings of others? You can ask your guides and higher
self to take it easy and not overwhelm you, however.
There is some reason this is one of your specialties. There
is an upside to feeling another's feelings. There is joy and
immense love to be felt as well as the darker emotions.
I've found myself in tears when someone's deceased
mother or child has shown up in a reading to say hello
to their loved ones and I can feel the immense love coming from them.

Psychic Laundry List

In this chapter's exercise, we bolster our road trip confidence. We'll find out just how crazy this trip looks, how talented we really are with navigation tools, and then we'll tell someone else all about it.

1. Are you afraid you will look crazy if you do this stuff? What looks and feels crazy to you when it comes to being psychic?

2. Journal assignment: What natural psychic abilities have you had since childhood? Do you remember shutting them down? What psychic abilities stayed with you or have reemerged since you became an adult?

3. Tell two people you trust that you are psychic. Ask for help before you do it. Call in your angels, fairies, and higher self for assistance. Then tell and see what happens.

✢✦Chapter 8✦✢
Fairies and You

This chapter will be short and sweet. Fairies, however, are not. Short maybe, but sweet, hardly. Have you seen that bumper sticker "Don't piss off the fairies"? I do a lot of work with them and they help me out a lot. If I don't include some information on them in this book, they're certain to get cranky. Fairies' big job is to teach you about taking risks for your soul. They frankly couldn't care less about how mad or uncomfortable that makes you or how sloppy and chaotic the process can be. They are not codependent. That makes them ruthless at coaching you. But they're also very funny, in a cynical way. One time they were telling a friend of mine that it was a good thing she was tough with some of her acquaintances and clients. Their exact phrasing was "Ferocity, you complete me." They are just ridiculous at times. But they do seem to know their stuff.

They are fluttering around you right now. They do the darnedest things to get your attention. They're practical jokers, keepers of the flame of creativity and spontaneity, and they especially love nature. Feel them flickering around the children when you're at the park. On my website, there is a picture of a Girl Scout trip my daughter and her troop took to a park in Los Angeles. As a Christmas service project, they decorated a tree with food for the wild animals. I could feel the fairies all around them while we were there. When I got the picture back, there were fairy orbs all around them. It was wonderful and amazing.

Fairies absolutely love to work with you on your illusions about control. The more you insist on your life or the people in it being a certain way, the more the fairies will nudge you to loosen your grip. They'll trip you up, slow you down, and masterfully make items go missing. Sticking to any form of a plan bores them to tears. They want you to have fun and not worry. They can't understand why humans are so overly invested in controlling outcomes. They wonder, whatever happened to enjoying a surprise ending?

Fairies will interrupt you from doing too much. They will cause chaos to prevent you from going into control-freak mode. They know our divine aspect lets go and lets God, and to that they say, let's party! Fairies allow you to laugh at yourself. They help you take a look at where you try to control all the details and invite you to give the fairies some breathing room to play.

If you're curious about the fairy creatures assigned to you, close your eyes and ask them to show themselves for one week. See what important items go missing. Watch for other signs, chaos, and balls of light. Honestly, it's quite a sight!

Nanette's Story

Yesterday I went out to this rock surrounded by tidal pools on the beach in Victoria, British Columbia. I asked the fairies to surprise me. Nothing happened. I started looking around me. At first I didn't see much, just barnacles and seaweed. Then I looked closer. I found some sea snails and some sea anemones. Tiny crabs crawled into the shade and damp provided by the seaweed. I touched the barnacles. They snapped their mouths closed and locked their bodies in place. I became fascinated with barnacles, beings I never saw before as more than sharp, painful nuisances. I spent an hour and a half just sitting in one spot, observing these tiny creatures and their world—a supreme accomplishment for someone who can't work for longer than fifteen minutes without her e-mail . . . I realized that it's not that I can't focus, it's that I can't focus on things that don't interest me.

So, barnacles, is it? I decided to go home and read up on them. I've always had this secret desire to be a biologist. "Maybe I should go back to school and study tidal pools," I thought. "Is that how the fairies are trying to surprise me?" I got into the car, turned on the radio, and a Seattle public radio broadcast was on. They were interviewing someone from the Seattle Aquarium who trained naturalists to educate the public about—you guessed it—tidal pools. And she then proceeded to talk barnacles for five minutes.

What exactly is/are the universe/fairies trying to tell me? Not sure yet. But they're trying to tell me something. And I might just start by signing up to become a beach naturalist next year in my new home of Seattle. Great assignment.

Ask the fairies to make their presence in your life known to you, and tell them you are willing to be surprised. This is about truly releasing thought forms (the way the ego thinks things should be) and outcomes. The fairies are master teachers at this. If things disappear for a while, 'tis a sure sign the fairies were here. If magic sparkles turn a situation completely around, 'tis the work of the winged ones. That's why they like dryers so much. Dryers turn things around! So do fairies! (They just told me that.) Also, if a fairy charm, bracelet, pillow, or picture comes into your realm, buy it. You're on fairy orders to indulge yourself. Fairies themselves don't spend money, but they sure can help you get it and spend it. Only in their world, it's more fun to buy it on credit first! Then when you get the money to back it up, you get extra credit because you took it on fairy faith! (They just told me that, too.) Also, call in all the specialist fairies you can think of. I have a parking fairy I've used for years in L.A. who creates miraculous spaces. There are health fairies, fun fairies, nature fairies, trip fairies, and the list goes on and on. Call in the specialists and watch the good times roll! One little note: Fairies do pull pranks. And sometimes they make you mad. But it's all part of the process, they promise.

Years ago there was a wonderful woman who worked at a local deli in northern California. Her name was Peggy and she always had a purple streak in her hair. She had lots of fairy energy around her. One day she was making me a chocolate shake and dumped it upside down. Her coworker just looked at her in disbelief because Peggy didn't spill often and was incredibly adept at all she did. But Peggy laughed and said, "Lorraine's fairy made me spill it." I knew she was right. I knew at least one of my fairies was on the prowl causing trouble. Fairy fun means chaos. They love to make things imperfect for a good laugh first and foremost. Peggy's comment also told me she really did see and get fairies, no question.

Psychic Laundry List

These exercises bring you nature and nurture fairy-style.

1. It's time for a fairy session! This requires you to go outside to someplace new. Ask the fairies to make their presence in your life known to you, and tell them you are willing to be surprised. It may be a city park, a country setting, or the beach. Get still, close your eyes, and relax. See what insights you get from your fairy friends and journal about it later.

2. Fairies cause mishaps to upset the order and cause chaos. They basically dynamite certain rigid thought patterns. Make a list of recent apparent mishaps. Did you lose your keys? Has something else been misplaced? Did something spill at a crucial time? Have certain plans been interrupted by something unexpected?

3. Stay awake this week for fairy activities and put on your fairy glasses to reexamine possible fairy activity in your past. Remember, fairies will cause chaos to prevent you from going into control-freak mode. Journal about whatever you discover.

✝✝Chapter 9✝✝
Let Go, Let God,
and Face the Music

You can go a long way down the psychic roadway and then discover you have screwed-up perceptions. You can also be in the middle of your road trip and realize your inner control freak decided to jump in and take a wrong turn. Rather than witness a scary moment during the trip, your ego acted out of fear to try to control the situation. And finally, you might also find out that you are seriously "should" challenged. Instead of kicking back and enjoying the ride with divine, you're worrying at every turn about whether you did it right. In this chapter, we'll check out our perceptions, see if we're really willing to go with the flow, and find out how much we "should" ourselves.

God of Truth

> *For here we are not afraid to follow*
> *truth wherever it may lead.*
> —*Thomas Jefferson*

A dame that knows the ropes isn't likely to get tied up.
—*Mae West*

I learned the following prayer from another psychic. Just seven words, it packs a punch and instantaneous results: "May the God of truth speak freely." You're essentially asking God and the universe to show you the truth when you feel confused.

The deal with this journey is that it's often like finding your way from one building to another using snow ropes. You have to feel your way through it. Most of what your intellect tells you is probably not the complete picture. We're trained to hear people's words and believe them, not size them up by their actions and the feel of their energy. When something feels bad to your gut, it probably is. The same goes for when something feels right. Your gut feeling can guide you down some slippery slopes.

When your emotional buttons are getting pushed and you feel like you have to *do something immediately,* that's a good time to back off and ask for help in seeing the situation clearly. Often you're confused for some very good reasons. Confusion slows you down. It keeps you from doing something idiotic until you can get clear about the situation. If you're using snow ropes, you're using them because it is clear to you that you need to get to the next building during the snowstorm. Look for the symbolism. Notice a person's actions or the details of a situation about which you're asking for truth. If you feel yourself pulling away from a friend, ask what evidence there is to back up your feelings of wanting or needing distance. Do they call you or are you always reaching out to them? Do the two of you have honest talks about your feelings? Is there a healthy exchange of time, energy, and listening or is it often lopsided? Are they honest or have you caught them in white lies? Do their gifts to you reflect their understanding of you? Or are they last-minute careless trinkets?

When you say the prayer "May the God of truth speak freely," expect a good look. The person will likely do something to indicate their true nature within days of your saying the prayer, but you have to stay awake to see it. I recommend journaling about patterns you experience in their behaviors and attitudes. God will give you the truth on a silver platter if you pray for it and listen to the answer.

So many of us are trapped under veils of misperceptions. We want to believe that the media, our church, our friends, and our extended family members tell us the truth. Are you willing to take a good hard look and see what's really going on? People and institutions that are self-serving and manipulative love those of us who refuse to lift the veil and look at the truth. It's the basis of all propaganda. That institution is betting on the public's willingness to believe the illusion. It's based on your assumption that the person or institution deserves your trust. Rather than making that person or organization earn your trust, you give it willingly. Then years down the road when everything about the relationship feels wrong and inside you feel betrayed, you feel shattered and confused. Even then it is difficult to see that you never forced these outsiders to earn your trust.

Trust is an earned commodity, not a given. It is a privilege to be trusted, not a right. If all of us got real and examined our relationships with one another, the media, the church, and our government leaders, we'd probably be quick to see that we've given unearned trust. I know it sounds cynical, but only when you're willing to see what's really out there can you begin to build the foundation of real love and energy exchange. Women in abusive relationships often believe the abuser loves them. It is only after they escape the relationship and move on to a more healthy partnership that they are able to see what real love looks like.

As a former investigative reporter, I was always a skeptic. But after I became psychic, my vision opened up. During my career, I had many sources inside the government. I now look back and see how many of the sources manipulated me to get their side of the story into the news. Many of the story subjects were tried in the media before they ever had their day in court. I trusted these sources to do the right thing because of their positions in government, but I now see how much I was manipulated by the stories they planted with me as a reporter. Now when I watch and read the news, it is plain as day to me how often the media is manipulated by the government and corporations. When I want to know the truth about something, I say the prayer "May the God of truth speak freely," and inevitably, something crosses my path via the Internet, a book, or a person I'm talking to that reveals the underlying truth.

The same goes for people and relationships. After my divorce, I was seeing a man who I didn't always believe was telling me the truth. I prayed that I would know the truth. Lo and behold, a girlfriend from another state told me this man had met with another woman one weekend when he had said he was out with friends. It turned out that my friend was a friend of the woman he had met with. My friend told me, not realizing I was romantically involved with him. My angels were having none of it. And after that, neither was I. I soon stopped seeing him.

I'm not saying seeing the truth is always pretty, but it can begin a stripping-away process that is essential to building a new platform for your life. The new platform is one built on real perceptions and integrity. It takes true grit to be willing to see the truth, however. That is one big reason so many are addicted to seeing things that aren't there and giving away their trust. It's hard to see that some people and institutions really don't have your interests at heart. That's why you need strong advocates you can trust—such as you, your higher self, and your guides. When you start with that support, it isn't as scary to get honest with yourself about who and what you're surrounded by. As you allow the God of truth to make itself known in your life, you find yourself increasingly surrounded by lovely people and equally loving environments. It requires that some changes be made, but making those changes allows more light and love into your life. Then when you look around, what you see is really what you get.

Molly's Story

One thing I'm finding is this sense that maybe I'm losing my mind because the more I tune into people's energy, the more I notice when it matches or doesn't match their words and/or actions. Like they're telling me one thing and their energy is screaming the opposite. It's like adding 1 + 1 and getting 3, which sometimes wreaks havoc with my sanity; self-doubt creeps in that I'm being paranoid and should just take people at their word. I use that prayer you mentioned: Let the God of Truth speak freely.

I received a reading ages ago, talking about life as a chessboard, black and white (lightness and darkness), needing to plan several moves in advance, etc. I'm starting to think this game of chess is like an integration of the soul's journey with the physical journey. When I live in the moment, that place of true power, it's like the next chess move just makes itself obvious.

Can I Get a Witness?

Really seeing is powerful. Really allowing is the ultimate form of grace. You're allowing the universe to work its magic by simply sidestepping the issue at hand and becoming more of a witness. Yang is masculine energy. Out of balance, it often tries to control and manage. In balance, it gets things done. Yin is the softer, more feminine energy. Yin allows. When yin is allowed her full say in your life, there's a synchronicity. When yang follows yin's guidance, there is magic. That is yin and yang in balance. Out of balance, true power turns into forced situations. Controlling people use force. Force doesn't allow for free choice and surprise solutions.

I've forced many situations, sometimes following what seemed like the right thing to do. Trying to be the nice guy is something I've excelled at. Trying to be nice when you don't feel nice can be a form of self-abuse. If your body and intuition are telling you to create distance from someone, even if you have to seem mean to do it, chances are it's for your own well-being and protection. The allowing nature of yin asks that you follow your gut. It asks that you be seemingly mean or rude to someone if it's in the flow. In a tricky way, trying to be nice can be your ego's way of trying to control a situation. Becoming a witness to your body's response and following its lead is very yin. Yin does not mean being a doormat. Yin allows. And allowing might mean appearing rude or abrupt to set your boundaries. If you're having a gut reaction that says "No!" then let it in and honor it.

"No" is a very yin, feminine word. It stops you and others from stepping on boundaries. Yin trusts. She believes in positive outcomes despite what look like difficult circumstances. Yin allows you to follow your biggest dreams and fantasies for your life. She opens the door to self-care. Envisioning the life you want and fine-tuning the life you have is one of her specialties. Psychic ability is fancy talk for living a life of yin and yang in balance. Yin is scary because she feels vulnerable, but that is also your greatest strength. Through yin the sacred feminine whispers the truth to you. The gentle voices of your higher self and angels intervene on your behalf to protect and guide you. They're most often heard in the quiet. They're seen in the magic results in your life.

The changes you fear the most also hold your greatest power. Just behind the whispers to make these changes is the force that empowers you to live in freedom.

Freedom and the Word "Should"

I've learned that "should" is a dangerous word. It usually comes from my ego, which thinks it knows best for my higher plan and knows best for others. Since I've been living by divine guidance, I've been pulling Spider-Man moves and walking upside down on the ceiling. As I wrote this, a buck poked his head through my office doorway and looked at me! Here's the point: You really do have to be willing to release everything, including all the shoulds. I spent so many years holding on to what I perceived as the "right form." My life has turned completely upside down in the past five years. And you know what? I'm absolutely better for it. It's been hard. It's meant cutting many codependent ties. I've cried, and I've had to lean on my guides, husband, and friends for a helluva lot of support. But here I am. And I feel freer this year than ever before.

Helen's Story Continued

Three years ago, Spirit was making it clear that I needed to leave my job. This, again, was unthinkable for my ego. How would I live? My salary was very significant to our household budget and art therapy jobs don't grow on trees. Besides, I was getting older and wouldn't it just make sense to stay here until I could retire? And don't forget about the health insurance! (At that point, a small voice in my head said, "If you stay, you will most certainly need your health insurance!") Well, talk about being resistant to Spirit's urgings. I simply could not make myself do it. It looked like financial suicide and how would I ever explain this choice to my husband? I simply refused to do it until I had direct and undeniable guidance to do so.

Naturally, Spirit responded to my invitation for direct guidance and I had two significant dreams in the same weekend that made it utterly clear that I was to take the road less traveled. As a matter of fact, one of the dreams had me driving into a huge freeway construction zone with the Black Madonna in the passenger seat. My experience of the Black Madonna is that she doesn't show up unless you are about to really get off the true track of your life. In the dream, she did not coddle me one bit, but told me I was already late for my next step! I was mortified and moved closer to trusting this guidance even though I was utterly blind to what it was going to bring to my life. Ultimately, I simply could not defy a direct order from Heaven. Spirit also supported me in telling my husband and so forth. I quit my job.

This was quite disorienting and I continued to feel like Spirit was doing nothing but taking things away from me. Walking the spiritual path is not for the fainthearted! It took a few months, but I began to see how my job was a major addiction for my ego. It was the last holdout in unplugging from my previous life. I kept expecting my husband to leave me and run for the hills, but he stayed with me. (Wouldn't you like to hear his side of it?) I spent hours sitting and stitching quietly on my art works. I began making more sophisticated accessories like purses, French cuffs, and scarves that were royally embellished. I learned some jewelry techniques and began sewing Swarovski crystals on my work. At first I was horrified at the cost of the crystals and the other materials I intuited to purchase. I think of this time as the "stitching for sanity" period.

I just kept making my art. But this is really when I became a Psychic Housewife. Here I was, not working outside the home for the first time in my life and I was not very comfortable with the whole idea. But I've gained a new understanding of how sacred providing a "home" for family to access is. Until this point in my life, I had not noticed this or actually even devalued it. I can see Spirit's work in balancing me. I entered an art event at our local textile center and was accepted.

I've given up trying to figure out what is going on in my life and how the story will end. I have absolutely no idea. All I know is that I wouldn't trade any of it for anything in the world. Being in conscious contact with Spirit and fellow sojourners is a magical way to live.

Psychic Laundry List

In this chapter's exercises, we're putting on our X-ray vision glasses, taking our feet off the brakes, and running down any "should" that we see on the road.

1. It's time to find out if your perceptions are screwed up or if you're really seeing clearly. Say the prayer "May the God of Truth speak freely" and see what gives this week. What are people's words and deeds telling you about them? What are the words and actions of government and business leaders showing you? Journal your insights.

2. What current circumstances or people in your life are you trying to control? What do you find scary about letting the flow happen?

3. List (at least) five "should" beliefs on a piece of paper. You might also include any "shoulds" that are perhaps coming up about your spiritual or psychic journey. Bless and thank your ego for assisting. Then do a releasing ritual. Put your list of "shoulds" in a pot outside and burn it.

✛Chapter 10✛
Frustration, Foolishness, and Foolhardy Fun

There may be a few *F* words you're feeling like throwing around about now. Let's go with the four in the chapter title. Here we'll deal with the frustrations and foolish feelings that emerge as we proceed further on our divine road trip. You might ask: Is there any relief for these feelings? There is. Your rest stops happen when you make time for creativity and fun. As a psychic housewife, it's important to stay current about where you're at, how you feel, and how you're planning to have some fun to get relief. If this journey is making you mad as hell, then yell about it. If you feel like a complete idiot, by all means say so. But for heaven's sake, don't lose your all-important ability to be silly, throw a good party, or make some really average art.

I'm Not Getting It!

Go ahead and be frustrated if you feel like you're not psychic, not making time for the exercises, or not understanding what you see and hear in the meditations. Just please also try to be gentle with yourself. If you felt like you were a full-blown psychic, you probably wouldn't be reading this book. My intention and that of your guides is to quietly get you to start thinking like a psychic and see what happens for you. I guarantee you that all of you have amazing capabilities in these matters. Psychic information is very soft, loving, and often funny. It's also concise. If it's so simple that you don't get it, ask for more info or let it go for now. What really matters is that you're carving out time for the exercises. I know it can be frustrating. I went from wallowing around in confusion to eventually demanding frequent clarification from the guides. But it took me a long time to get there. Go easy, it will come in. It just might not look like what your ego is expecting! That's the trick of the divine—it doesn't bow to the ego's expectations. In fact, if it's frustrating to your ego, that's another sure sign that it's coming from someplace outside your personality. Remember, it takes grit to make a pearl.

School of the Fool

Here's one of the really sucky parts of this journey: playing the fool. It's humbling, it's painful, and it's fundamental to really, truly embracing your divinity. How many, many times I've heard the call to the Lord and it sounded like nails on chalkboard.

A mentor and psychic friend tells a story of being on a double date when she was in her twenties. An angel told her the woman next to her needed a healing on her heart (for a physical ailment). "No, no," she was thinking, "this will bring down the whole date." The young psychic looked out the window and said, "F#!K you, God!" But she did the healing anyway and she told the group exactly what she was doing. It turned out the young woman did have a heart problem that was healed. But my friend never heard from her date again.

Looking ridiculous is all part of this deal. Being *willing* to look ridiculous is an even bigger part. The willingness to play the fool can go a long way in battling the evil of the ego. What do I mean by that? When you stop trying to prove or perform for ego's sake and relax and let go, you stop resisting. I've said I'm sorry to adversaries who I knew had very bad intentions. I apologized because I knew I needed to for myself. You know what happens when you apologize to someone who loves to hold power over people? They gloat. They don't say, "Oh, that's all right. I accept your apology." They say, "Well, I'm thrilled you see how wrong you are, because what you did really was terrible." At that point, I want to yell, but I sit there, willing to eat humble pie. I know if revenge is in order, it's in the hands of the Lord.

In situations of humbling yourself, your ego self typically wants to resort to fight or flight. You'll either want to apologize and then punch them in the face if they don't respond well, or apologize and then run. Unfortunately, sometimes you have to apologize to complete idiots to stay in your full integrity and you can feel very foolish doing so. What's worse, punching them or running away from them afterward isn't high on the divine to-do list. Standing there humbly and listening to whatever they say in response is.

As with my psychic friend on the double date, the other way to play the fool is to follow your guidance and intuition without explaining. You just do what you know you are compelled to do and you don't explain. How uncomfortable is that? Here are some examples:

quitting your job when your family is already short on cash, dropping out of the volunteer parent group when they really need help, and buying a motorcycle or convertible when the kid's day-care bill is due. Now try all that without explaining yourself to your wary-eyed family, friends, and neighbors. Most masters don't explain themselves much. They're not terribly apologetic for any of their choices. Centered people dare to look selfish when they are actually operating under the premise of self-care and divine direction. But from the outside looking in, this can look awful. If you're the person who looks selfish, it can also feel really icky.

This journey is not about always feeling good or comfortable. You can feel really, really awful while doing some really, really good things. Most of us haven't been trained in self-care; we've been trained in guilt. It's much easier to go to beating yourself up than to praise yourself for doing something that society deems wrong. But if your heart is guiding you forward, it's probably an essential part of your steppingstone to divine.

Feel embarrassed? Get used to it. Feel afraid? You're right on track. Feeling horribly uncomfortable? Sounds like you're exactly where you are supposed to be.

Somewhere along the way we've been taught we're supposed to feel good when we follow divine. It just isn't the case. In the twelve steps of Alcoholics Anonymous, it's suggested that the alcoholic humbly admit he or she is powerless over alcohol. That takes some humility, but the willingness to look foolish, like someone who has succumbed to addiction, is the linchpin for success in the program. Another aspect of the program is sharing with another person your inventory of character defects. Again, that entails a huge surrender to looking foolish.

It seems divine can't come in for a complete landing without humility. The ego is put on ice while the entire you goes out on a limb and looks ridiculous. The ego may squawk, but your job is to allow light into places that look weak, wrong, or embarrassing. Of course, you have free choice; you can avoid looking foolish by doing what you feel you "should" do instead of what your heart says you "must" do. But there is immense freedom on the other side of playing the fool. As you keep releasing the bondage of "looking good" to society, you unleash the true you, the divine you. If you can come to the other side of these experiences and have a good laugh, you've earned your achievement certificate from the School of the Fool. The only catch is that you never graduate.

Creativity and Fun

"What the hell? Why did I sign up for this anyway?" I can hear you saying. "The journey just keeps getting stranger and most of the time I barely know what's going on." Must be time for some serious fun. Silliness, creativity, and fun activities can offer relief on the psychic housewife journey. Dare to look ridiculous in public and in front of your kids, be willing to make some really iffy art, and consider going for a ride in a convertible or on a horse or motorcycle. "What are you talking about, Lorraine? Is this a sneaky way of suggesting even more self-care?" Yep. Creativity and fun are sophisticated ways to take care of yourself on the psychic housewife journey. If your head's in the stars, why not put your feet on the pegs of a motorcycle or into some stirrups? Last week I pulled up the Harley Davidson website. What's their current ad campaign? "Screw it, let's ride." Sounds good to me (and your guides like the notion as well).

I've had the privilege of knowing several artists very well over the past decade. They have an amazing ability to create without expectations. They get materials. They start painting, gluing, building, videotaping, or writing. There's no agenda about selling it or mass-producing it. I'm not saying they don't experience challenges with the ego, but for the most part they really enjoy the process. As time has gone on, I've found myself buying more painting and drawing materials and more musical instruments to have around the house, using my cameras to create fun videos, and doing creative writing. My husband says something brilliant about our American society today. He believes that the last bastion of creativity that's condoned here is our ability to shop for products we desire. Our environment doesn't always encourage the true essence of creativity. But if you think of God as creator and yourself as imbued with spirit, it follows you're inclined to create.

For me, creativity has become a pressure release valve for all that I psychically see and feel going on in my life around me. I see my kids light up when they are painting or playing music. It's fun! And on that topic—expressing joy is essential. It's often too easy to stump some of my clients by asking them one single question: What are you doing for fun? Answers range from working out to reading a good book. OK, but I mean fun. That involves hearty laughter or a smile glued to your face. Fun comes to you when you simply ask the universe for it. It turns out there isn't much planning involved.

I spend time with my friends, I go for a motorcycle ride with my husband, a convertible comes into my life, I take an unexpected trip to the mountains or the beach, or I go to a rock concert. With three kids around, I'm still thrilled to go to the movies with my family or just my husband. Sometimes, fun does come in a simple form, and it's not about being busy or achieving. It's about feeling light and airy. This is an important aspect of the journey. You don't need to work on yourself or your life 24/7. Often when you let go and let God, that's when the miracles can come in from left field. It's trusting that while you're off enjoying yourself, the universe is still working on your behalf. Next time we talk, don't let me stump you with my favorite question: What are you doing to have fun?

Psychic Laundry List

In this chapter, we work through our feelings of frustration and foolishness. Then we have some foolhardy fun.

1. Put on your boxing gloves, it's time to fight with your guides. I mean it. If there's anything you're really angry or upset about regarding their recent divine guidance or lack thereof, let them have it.

2. When was the last time you humbly had to admit you were addicted to something, just plain wrong, or that you needed help? In what areas of your life do you feel you need to do that again? Journal about it, then make an action plan to ask humbly for help from your angels, friends, counselor, or a 12-step program.

3. What about this psychic journey makes you feel foolish?

4. Next time you do self-care or something psychic, don't explain it to anyone—just do it. Journal the reaction from a wary friend, your mother-in-law, or whoever seems to be judging your choices.

5. Is there a shortcut to some simple daily fun and creativity? Do you need a bicycle? A motorcycle? Regular hikes with a friend? Art supplies? Pick one and make it an action step. Ask your angels to help make it a reality in your life.

✛✛Chapter 11✛✛
Doing Readings

Now that we've had a ton of fun applying psychic concepts to ourselves and our lives, let's experiment with others. Put on your lab coats, everyone! It's time to see if these formulas work! One of the most interesting and informative parts of our psychic housewives online class is when women begin to give each other psychic readings. At first they're terrified, then they're affirmed. It's amazing to witness these women exchange accurate psychic information with each other. I've watched friends and clients jump with both feet into doing readings and the results have been truly mind-boggling. There's no way to know if these exercises work, unless you hang your "psychic" shingle for at least a few friends or family members. Stumbling through the imagery and sensations, experiencing the visceral sensation of guides communicating through you, and finding out how your "clients" react can be incredibly nerve-wracking and also very affirming. This is the exercise that seals the deal. It's the culmination of your hard work doing the psychic housewife exercises. It's the surefire way to discover the beauty and intensity of your psychic abilities. Only in this way can you experience the immense vulnerability and power that come with using this gift. As you exercise this muscle, you gain experience and begin to trust the guides and their imagery, feelings, and words. It is an amazing way to be of service, but it requires the humility to flounder a bit while you do it.

What happens when you give someone a psychic reading? As the psychic, you open yourself up to receiving images and information from them about their thoughts, their job, their family, and their soul's journey. Another aspect of a reading can be hearing from the person's deceased relatives or pets. You may also hear directly from the person's spirit guides who love to weigh in during a reading.

Sometimes getting started can be the hardest part. Using angel or fairy divination decks can help you connect to certain aspects of the person so the reading can continue. If you're with them in person, have them pull a card or two to get started. If you're giving them a reading over the phone, pull a few cards yourself for them. For some psychics, the divine information about your client may need time to land. One of my psychic friends takes questions from people and the information usually comes in for her a day or two following. Do not pressure yourself to "get" anything in a certain way. Do follow your intuition to a method that feels easy and somewhat effortless. It's important not to feel strained or stressed while giving someone a reading.

When I first started doing readings, I encountered a range of clientele and their messengers from the other side. There were complete nimrods, wonderful people, freaky spirits, and gentle ones. When I first opened up, I gave everyone readings. Now I'm fussy about it and so are my guides. I'm also fussy about other people's messengers. Frankly, some of them can be downright mean and rude. Others are mature and thrilled to have your help in giving their person a message. I highly recommend you ask your own guide to act as a go-between, and to warn you if the reading is coming from a low vibration or is draining to you. I'm going to offer a few more tips. Again, they're suggestions only; it's up to you to experiment and figure out what techniques work for you.

Reading Starter Tips

Use a pendulum to check if it is the highest good for you to give a reading to a certain person. If you get a no, the timing may be wrong or you two may not be a fit for each other.

If you get a yes, then clear with sage or frankincense the area where you'll be doing the reading (even when you're doing the reading over the phone).

Say an invocation out loud for you and your client as you begin the reading. Pray to bring in your guides of highest consciousness as well as your client's. Then ask for help from the client's deceased relatives and crystal allies that are willing and able to assist.

Set an intention to receive information that aligns the client's ego with their soul.

Again, praying out loud, ask that the reading be done in divine right order with full protection, and close the prayer by saying "and so it is."

Saying this out loud sets the intention of the reading to be a divine experience. It also reminds you that you are not doing this yourself, that it is divine energy moving through you. The protection request asks the guides to stop interference by someone who might want to stop the reading. For example, if a client wants to know if she should stay away from her ex-boyfriend, that man's soul might try to interrupt the reading. A word to the wise: If you feel interrupted by an outside entity several times or your phone malfunctions, don't try to power through the reading. It's likely a sign to end the session.

If no clear information seems to be coming into you, simply stop the reading and tell your friend/client this isn't a good time. I have learned the hard way that if I'm straining to get the information, it means I'm forcing the reading to happen. That can be a huge energy drain. There are several reasons you might not get the information. Sometimes you're simply not meant to receive it, your guides may be guarding you against negative energy, or the client may be afraid to receive the psychic information.

It's important that you and the person receiving the reading ground into the earth and relax as much as possible. By grounding, I mean have your friend/client turn off computers in the room, have them try to clear their heads from nervous chatter, and if necessary, have them sit on the floor. It's a good idea for you to follow similar guidelines. Giving readings near electronics is a bad idea. Electronic devices put out frenetic energy that can disrupt psychic signals.

See if you get any images, hear any words, or see any details about their lives. Again, you might wish to work from a deck of cards to get started. Often you'll receive general images that lead to concise messages from the client's higher self, their guides, or deceased relatives. Some psychics only hear deceased relatives and friends, while others hear only spirit guides.

If you're using a pendulum for yourself, you might want to use one while attempting readings. Sometimes the pendulum will give a clear-cut yes or no answer to a question that your brain feels confused about. It's a good idea to have a personal pendulum and one to practice with during readings. That way you don't mix your personal energies with your friend/client's aura.

When you're first starting out, there's no need to overdo it. If you get information that seems scary or too personal about your client, just keep it to yourself. It takes time to learn how to be discerning. Not everyone wants to hear gory details about their past, present, or future. It's not your job to be the sole source of information for anyone. They have plenty of soul sources, and it's up to them to find them. Just play with this and keep it as light as you can when you first do readings. Taking a playful, light approach helps ease everyone's nerves when you are a newly minted psychic.

At the end of the reading, say out loud that if you and your volunteer client have exchanged any energy, that energy be returned to its original state and ownership. (This is a way to keep from becoming energetically entangled with your client.)

Say a closing prayer (which I fondly call an "out-vocation"), repeating most of what you said at the beginning about divine right order and full protection, and then give thanks for the reading and the information and love contained in it.

Sometimes the reading you give won't make complete sense to your client at the time. Here's an example from one of my early psychic readings. I told a client that her deceased father (an avid golfer) was making contact. I saw a man in a tweed hat with 1930s golfing gear. She seemed confused by the image and I felt unsettled because it seemed that the information wasn't a fit at the time. Later that week, a forwarded golf catalog that was supposed to go to her father came to her house. It had a man on the front wearing a tweed cap with 1930s golfing gear. She e-mailed me and told me she understood it was a sign from her father.

The information I've given you in this chapter is just an explanation of how I do readings. Of course, you will develop a perfect process that suits you. Practice makes perfect, or something like that. You will find your own style and way. These are just my tips. When I use the word "client," I'm referring to the person to whom you are giving the reading. I'm not suggesting that you do paid readings at this point. The objective of the exercise is to become comfortable with doing readings for others. I suggest beginning with people you feel most comfortable with, who accept the existence of the psychic realm. That will make your venture into doing readings feel a lot safer. It's so important to take care of yourself throughout this process. Treat yourself like a newborn and go gently.

Psychic Laundry List

In these exercises, we take our new abilities out for a ride.

1. Remember what I said about the Butterflies Alive exhibit at the Living Desert? When a caterpillar forms a chrysalis, it forms it on the inside. So the caterpillar's head falls off in the process (no longer needed for eating leaves) and the butterfly bursts out of its former body. So how often are you letting your head fall off and just following your gut? Journal about something you've done based entirely on your gut feeling.

2. Find someone who is on a similar journey and offer to exchange psychic readings with that person. Follow the suggested guidelines in this chapter for giving a reading, along with any step you get intuitively for yourself. Give it a try. You may be surprised at how psychic you really are!

3. What happens when you get psychic information for someone and it proves to be accurate? Are you excited? Scared? Notice the way the information came into you and how you can expand on that in your day-to-day life. Did you receive images, hear words, or just have an inner knowing? This is a way to practice your abilities and also come to better understand how they work for you.

4. What information are you getting about people and situations around you? Write it in your psychic journal and see if you are provided with facts that back up your insights.

✦Chapter 12✦
Closing Thoughts

As I sit writing the final chapter of this book, it occurs to me now that my life seems so normal in the third dimension and so magical in the fourth dimension. We are living in a lovely home in a tree-lined neighborhood in Los Angeles. My kids are all enrolled in private school and doing beautifully. My husband is working as a video editor on the number one television show airing this summer and fall. Looking over our ups and downs these past few years, I can't believe how life has leveled out and become so amazingly wonderful. I had a professional reading from a psychic last week who said she could not believe the amount of loving energy coming from our house and our family.

Just today we had an example of the synchronicity and power of our family and the universe. My preteen daughter was missing a boy she'd met at a local camp for teens. Her time was finished there, but his continued. The kids and I decided to take a metro train to downtown Los Angeles to play tourist. At the train station on our way back, the entire teen group from camp was getting onto the same train we were. My daughter got to see her friends and (don't tell her I told you) the boy she has a crush on. I turned to my oldest son and said, "What are the chances of this happening?" He couldn't believe it either. Five minutes of timing difference and we would have missed them. I told my daughter she did a great job manifesting and I'm sure all of us were working with her on some level to make sure we made it to the train platform on time! Just last week I thought of taking my son to the L.A. Zoo. But somehow it didn't feel right. That evening I learned there had been a brush fire at Griffith Park and the entire zoo had been evacuated.

Also this week, I heard my daughter talking to her girlfriend. Her friend said, "I thought I was your best friend!" My daughter replied, "You're my second to best friend. My mom is my best friend. I tell her everything." After all that has passed between my daughter and me and in my own life, these words went right to the bone. I tear up thinking of them now. And I know her words are the direct result of a lot of work I've done on allowing spirit to mother through me. It was another affirmation that these principles really do work when you work them in your life.

Spirit never asks you to prove your worthiness for love and abundance. Spirit does ask you to prove your willingness to receive it. This journey is about releasing rigid ego forms and replacing them with overflowing divinity. It is not, however, a journey for wimps.

It takes love, patience, and a tremendous amount of faith to build this platform. It also takes a lot of heavenly help. You might experience great heartbreak on this journey, immense financial insecurity, and the feeling that you are going crazy. But when you're in your rocking chair, on your front porch at age ninety, you'll be able to look back and say, "I took risks for my soul." A life based on divine guidance is one worth living. Our higher self always pushes us toward expansion, toward more freedom of choice, toward more trust of divine timing, and toward authentic relationships. It feels, well, divine!

Friends and clients have surrendered to their psychic abilities and a life of divine guidance. They've quit jobs and careers, their relationships have changed or transformed, and they've moved across the country or to the other side of the world. I watch now with awe and wonder as they find new loving communities, discover amazing and loving partners, and find creative and exciting ways to bring in money. Sometimes the changes have been big and bold, sometimes slow and uneven. But the results are irrefutable. This stuff really does work, though not usually on our ego's timeline or with our ego's methodology.

If it is true you have to go through hell to get to heaven, then so be it! My guides keep telling me this life can be effortless when I let go and let God. But you know what? It did take a lot of effort to get to the effortless part. If you're tempted to skip the exercises in the book, please don't. That's your ego's attempt to stop psychic flow. The guides and I have designed this book to help you create results that prove you really are psychic, and that when you do your self-care, everyone benefits. It was also written to help you build a community of kindred spirits.

This book has been expanded and shaped by my good friend Annelise Christ. Annelise has been a longtime friend and was also a psychic student of mine. She has graciously used her skills and her life experiences to make this book more coherent. I trust her implicitly, because she models her faith in thought, word, and deed. To borrow a phrase from a program I like, she practices these principles in all her affairs.

Women out there are doing this stuff every day, getting results, and experiencing miracles. Psychic ability isn't reserved for certain people; it is available for people who are certain they want to connect consciously with divine. I'm convinced that if you've read this far into the book, you are one of those people. You are a blessed child of God. You are a psychic housewife!

Blessings, Lorraine

About the Author

LORRAINE ROE has been working as a professional psychic since 2002. She is a former investigative reporter and television producer. She won four News Emmys for her work.

Lorraine lives in Los Angeles with her husband and three children. They escape to their house in the woods of Northern California whenever possible.

Hampton Roads Publishing Company

... for the evolving human spirit

Hampton Roads Publishing Company
publishes books on a variety of subjects,
including spirituality, health,
and other related topics.

For a copy of our latest trade catalog,
call toll-free, 800-766-8009,
or send your name and address to:

HAMPTON ROADS PUBLISHING COMPANY, INC.
1125 STONEY RIDGE ROAD
CHARLOTTESVILLE, VA 22902
E-mail: hrpc@hrpub.com • Internet: www.hrpub.com